HARD LANDSCAPE IN BRICK

Cecil C. Handisyde

The Architectural Press Ltd
London

Foreword

This book describes the properties, choice and use of clay or calcium silicate brickwork. Background information is given first, followed by illustrations and general comments on the various uses of brickwork in the landscape. From page 39, technical information on materials and design is given for paving, steps, freestanding and retaining walls, and other landscape features. The information is based on data from the United Kingdom, while the Appendix on page 73 describes the applicability of this information to work in other countries. Examples from many countries have been used to illustrate the text.

Hard landscape in brick serves as a companion to *Hard landscape in concrete* by Michael Gage and Maritz Vandenberg (Architectural Press, 1975). As such, it avoids repetition of technical details of concrete work, such as the design of concrete bases beneath paving, which are applicable to finishes in either brick or concrete.

Metric measurements have been used, with conversion factors for imperial units being laid out in the Appendix.

Acknowledgements

The author would like to thank the many people who have helped with the preparation of this book, including a number of individual architects, brick manufacturers and engineers, as well as the Brick Development Association. He would like to acknowledge the following for use of illustrative material:
Bill Toomey
Ronald Adams
Leonard Manasseh
Ibstock Building Products
Carlsberg Brewery, Copenhagen
Shepherd Epstein & Hunter
Stillman & Eastwick Field
Farmer & Dark
De Nederlandse Baksteenindustrie
Colin Westwood
GLC Department of Architecture and Civic Design

ISBN 0 85139 283 0
First published in book form 1976
by The Architectural Press Ltd
© The Architectural Press Ltd 1976

Printed in Great Britain by
Diemer & Reynolds Ltd, Bedford

This book is to be returned on or before
the last date stamped below.

Contents

Part 1: The landscape

Chapter 1: Brick as a landscape material

1

1 Introduction

1.01 The term 'landscape' is commonly applied to areas where the dominant features are natural materials such as grass, crops, growing plants and trees and exposed earth or rock. The term 'hard landscape' may be variously interpreted. It might be considered as a town scene, consisting entirely or very largely of hard paved areas enclosed by buildings, **1**, **2**, or it might be interpreted as referring solely to paving. On the other hand, a single dominant feature, such as the viaduct in **3**, can form a dramatic part of an otherwise totally natural scene and so might merit inclusion in the term 'hard landscape'.

1.02 While taking account of the relationship of landscaping to nearby buildings, this book is directed primarily to aspects of brickwork when it is used in situations involving considerations different from those which apply to its use in normal building conditions.

1.03 While design should certainly not be regarded as a series of isolated exercises, eg buildings, pavings, planting etc, it is often necessary for practical purposes for the components of a total scene to be treated as almost separate parts of the whole. Sometimes landscaping may be an entirely separate design and construct operation, as for example in redesigning an

1 *Hard landscape as a tough finish in a tough situation (Hanover Trust Building, New York).*
2 *An all-brick composition where buildings, walls and* pavings are all hard but not harsh (Buddinge Church, Copenhagen).
3 *Hard feature in a soft landscape (Ouse Valley railway viaduct, Sussex).*

4

4

5

6

existing town area for pedestrian use without alteration to the buildings already there, **4**. Even where new buildings and their surroundings form a single scheme, the programming is such that landscape follows after most building work has been finished.

1.04 Where the ideal situation of single overall design responsibility occurs, the time factor still applies and there is likely to be a considerable gap between broad design of the 'landscape' and working out of details. Often the general designer will delegate the detailed work for which precise knowledge of technical aspects is recognised as necessary, but, as with other technical parts of any project, difficulties will occur at the detailing stage if the overall design is not based upon a good understanding of the main characteristics of the materials to be used. The general characteristics of brickwork, as used in buildings, are well documented and generally understood. Many of the same factors apply to brickwork used in landscaping but there are some important additional aspects to consider and it is essential for the effect of some of these to be taken into account when making early design decisions.

2 Reasons for use of brickwork in landscaping

2.01 When a questionnaire was sent to a number of architects, without exception they referred to appearance as their reason for choosing brick, and mentioned the attractiveness of the scale of brickwork. Almost all considered brick colour to be a major factor in their choice of material, and many referred to texture, either as a separate quality or as being linked with scale. There were also references to compatibility of materials with nearby buildings and to low maintenance cost.

3 Special functional requirements

3.01 The main uses of brickwork in landscaping are obviously for paving and walling. Functional requirements for incidental features are generally likely to be similar to those for walls.

Paving
3.02 External brick paving is subject to more severe wetting than most brickwork in buildings and is likely to be significantly wet for much longer periods of time. This, plus the cooling effect of exposure to heat loss by radiation to the cold night sky, makes high resistance to frost damage an essential quality. The dampness factor also brings in the question of possible visual defects from efflorescence and the need to consider the possibility of damage from sulphate attack.

3.03 The mechanical effect of traffic is also a factor that does not apply to brickwork in buildings. Overall wear may be of little or no importance in light pedestrian situations, **5**, or be an essential factor in the choice for a heavy duty road, **6**. It is not always an easy matter to judge the requirement for dense pedestrian use but from some examples in the United States it appears that there is sometimes a tendency to underestimate the effect of foot traffic, for example on pavements of main shopping streets in city centres, where a hard surfaced brick is necessary. Most bricks of a quality suitable for

external use are tough enough to withstand reasonably severe traffic, provided the bedding is well done and the base is appropriate to the traffic conditions.

3.04 Generally, the possibility of disfigurement by damage to brick arrises is more important than surface abrasion. Avoiding damage depends largely upon joint design, but it is worth noting that the most vulnerable area often occurs on front edges of steps.

3.05 A characteristic of normal building brickwork is its low maintenance cost. This also holds true for correctly designed brick paving, but one must recognise that disfigurement can occur. By far the most likely cause is poor workmanship during initial laying, mainly by splashing wet mortar without immediate and thorough cleaning off. Local disfigurement can occur from oil or grease staining, eg from waste containers standing outside institute or restaurant kitchens or on pavements in front of food shops. It is little satisfaction to know that most other types of material would suffer similarly. In the US there is a special hazard, not seriously present in Britain: almost impossible to remove, dark hard lumps of ejected chewing gum.

Freestanding walls
3.06 Freestanding walls are somewhat comparable to parapet walls of buildings, ie they must be designed to prevent water entry from the top, but, even with that precaution, exposure to wetting from both sides means more wetting than on normal building walls and a need to select appropriate quality materials.

3.07 For high freestanding walls or walls in exposed situations design must provide for appropriate strength against wind damage. This is a function of wall shape rather than brick strength. Lateral strength should also be considered in parapet walls, as with parapet walls on buildings.

Retaining walls
3.08 In addition to design of wall plus foundation for resistance to lateral loading, choice of material should recognise that unless full waterproofing is applied the quality of materials must be correct for a damp situation. Frost damage may be a slightly lower risk than for freestanding walls but the possible introduction of salts from adjacent earth should be considered.

Movement
3.09 Precautions against thermal and moisture movement are recognised as necessary in many ordinary building walls. Moisture movement is likely to be rather greater in freestanding walls. Thermal effect, resulting from different face exposures, may be slightly greater for freestanding walls than for building walls.

3.10 For paving, the day/night temperature differential is likely to be high, so, although minor cracks in pavings are not usually of great immediate importance, movement joints are necessary for extensive areas of mortar bedded paving.

4 The effect of functional requirements on choice of bricks

4.01 Satisfactory performance depends upon the choice of material, correct design and good workmanship. In the choice of bricks, by far the most important difference between ordinary facing brickwork in buildings and landscape work is the high exposure condition and consequent wetting to which pavings and many walls are exposed. For external paving and most walling, clay bricks should conform to the requirements of BS 3921 Part 2 special quality class. There are, however, some bricks which, while not meeting fully all of the BS special quality class requirements, have been found satisfactory. Advice from manufacturers or evidence that the bricks have given satisfactory service under conditions

4 *Redesigned urban area for pedestrian use (The Netherlands).*
5 *Tea on the terrace causes*
little wear and tear (garden at Fleet, Hampshire).
6 *Heavy duty roadway (Holland).*

7

similar to those proposed should be obtained if all the BS conditions are not met.

4.02 It is equally necessary for calcium silicate bricks to be of high quality. This will usually mean equal to or above a class 3 brick as defined by BS 187 Part 2.

4.03 More information on brick quality and specification will be found on page 41 'Selection of bricks'. Concrete bricks are not referred to, being covered in a companion volume, *Hard landscape in concrete*.

4.04 These quality requirements have an important design implication. One of the attractions of brickwork is that it can provide a continuity of treatment for buildings and their surroundings, **7, 8**. If a designer wishes to use precisely the same brick type for buildings and landscape works, the quality of material is likely to be governed by the requirements of the landscaping applications. This should be recognised sufficiently early in decision making for it to be taken into account when selecting the type of brick for the buildings. There is a risk that, in a rush to complete building design, the details of the landscaping work will be left for subsequent attention. The building brick chosen could then be found unsuitable for the outside works.

4.05 A cost aspect may arise in that, broadly, the high quality materials appropriate to high exposure conditions may be more costly than alternatives which could meet requirements for normal building. If the problem is recognised and the two requirements are jointly investigated, the wide choice of bricks available may well enable the designer to meet his objectives by using two different but harmonious types of brick. It is worth noting here that natural weathering quite often results in minor alterations in the appearance of materials in different parts of a building. Although an attractive characteristic of brickwork is that it 'grows old pleasantly', in most forms it is not immune to some change. Different exposure and weathering may be most likely to occur on paving and it might therefore be quite logical to choose a material which, from the start, does not attempt to match precisely any nearby walling.

8

7 *Continuity of material from building to paving (Oakland, California).*

8 *Continuity of material extended to sign feature (Oakland, California).*

5 Other general design considerations

5.01 Although the properties of brickwork are so well known, three aspects of its use in landscaping are worth stressing.

5.02 First, there are innumerable examples of the long and largely maintenance-free life of bricks in buildings. Equally, there is plenty of evidence of its ability to withstand the more rigorous conditions applying to landscape work, **9**.

5.03 Second, one aspect of durability that seems to be largely ignored in Britain is the feasibility of using brick for road finishes; this in spite of the fact that it has been used as a hard wearing, heavy duty flooring in industrial buildings. In The Netherlands its use for road finishes has been extensive, both for very heavy load conditions, **6**, and for lighter traffic situations, **10**.

5.04 Third, the scale of brickwork as a factor in appearance is referred to below, but the small size of unit provides valuable design flexibility. Even without the use of 'specials', the material is suited to radiused work, **11**, **12**. For paving, the small unit size allows awkward shapes to be covered without difficulty and without unpleasant interruption to overall pattern.

5.05 Reference was made earlier to designers appreciating brickwork for its appearance and especially for colour, texture and scale. All these are important and each interacts with the others, often to produce what might be described as a 'friendly' appearance. More will be said in later chapters about the effect of detailed design on appearance, but one general point worth mentioning here is the importance of viewpoint. Work which is seen mostly from afar or only briefly while travelling along a main traffic road can have very different design requirements from that which is regularly seen close at hand or where there is a need for compatibility between hard material and soft planting. No particular material is right for all situations and a design can often benefit by a judicious combination.

9

9 *Paving in a palace courtyard (Urbino, Italy).*
10 *Suburban roadway and pavement (Amersfoort, The Netherlands).*
11 *Curved walling simply constructed from standard small units (Villa Mariotti, Tivoli, Italy).*

10

11

12

6 New developments

6.01 As a traditional material brickwork has been gradually developed over thousands of years. In general development in recent years, brickmaking has largely changed from a relatively small-scale operation to a large-scale production process. Research has identified quality requirements, and present methods of manufacture, with good process control, make for more predictable performance and less variability in quality of a particular type.

6.02 New colours and textures are periodically introduced but two trends are particularly noteworthy. In recent years the fairly widespread use of perforated bricks has spread to Britain (see page 42). Calcium silicate bricks, increasingly used for buildings, have recently been employed for paving work.

6.03 Perhaps the most interesting new possibility is the feasibility of using pre-jointed brick pavers, **13**. For some years prefabricated brick wall panels have been the subject of considerable research and development. They have been used successfully in the US and Europe, and they are increasingly being used in Britain. Now it seems that a related process may be attractive for some paving. A development example is shown in **13** in which thin clay pavers, without any heavy concrete backing, have been laid, using panels of up to almost 1 m square. This development came about because of a significant alteration in contract procedure. Two problems tend to occur with paving work. The first is that for practical reasons paving is usually almost the last contract operation and in consequence must inevitably be done quickly. The second problem arises to some extent from the first: general contractors often find it difficult to provide sufficiently skilled labour to do good work of this kind quickly. Ordinary bricklayers, used to vertical work, are not always either capable of or particularly willing to tackle paving successfully. To meet this situation a 'supply and fix' service seems a reasonable proposition. This immediately brings together the manufacturing and the site processes with the chance of a really new look at a traditional job.

6.04 As part of this new-look process it was realised not only that greater speed on site would be welcome but also that one of the big problems with paving is to avoid disfigurement from mortar splashing or spreading over the brick surface. A successful use of pre-jointed units would make for speed and reduce the risk of disfigurement.

6.05 Simple rectangular pre-jointed units are clearly of most use for large areas of paving. Pre-jointed units to special shapes can be made but often the most sensible arrangement may be to combine the use of standard pre-jointed units with a limited amount of ordinary site laying.

13a

12 *Curved shapes in walls and pavings using standard units (Countesthorpe College Upper School).*
13a, b *Pre-jointed brick paver units combined with site fixed normal pavers (Ibstock Pre-cast Ltd).*

13b

Chapter 2: Landscape walls

1 Texture and geometry

1.01 Although unquestionably 'landscape', this monumental design at Carlsberg Brewery, Copenhagen, **1**, **2**, is the end wall of a factory. The site for a required new building was beside a large garden belonging to an important house occupied as a grace-and-favour residence. Objection to an industrial building at the end of the main vista was eventually withdrawn on agreement that the building could be designed as an acceptable addition to the landscape.

1.02 What could have been an overpowering mass has been reduced in scale by the breakdown into smaller areas, with each section clearly defined. Added interest and definition of the panels comes from the stepped treatment and from a subtle concave shaping to each section. All these factors are important to the effect as seen from afar, and especially from the house in question. The very heavy texture is also significant at distant viewing. The clean line of a metal damp course projecting below the brick-on-edge wall finish provides a good stop to the textured brickwork and plays a surprisingly important part in defining the panels.

1.03 Walking towards the wall, the character of the texture becomes more apparent and the scale of the brick units gradually becomes more obvious and prevents the overall size from being oppressive at close quarters.

In time, the simple tree planting at ground level will play a greater part in the total composition, and small trees and bushes planted at the several step-back levels will also modify the present effect.

1.04 In contrast to the previous example, Great Missenden Library has the simplest possible garden wall, seen only from close by, **3**. Material matches the adjacent building, scale is appropriate to its position and the bricks and jointing have a slightly rough appearance which complements the planting.

1 *Large scale feature wall at Carlsberg Brewery, Copenhagen.*
2 *Close-up of the brewery wall. Note the effect of viewing distance when* *compared with* **1**.
3 *Small scale, close viewing, with harmony between building, planting and simple wall (Great Missenden branch library).*

4

5

6

7

8

1.05 This traffic directing island at the Tara Hotel, London, is near enough to benefit from treatment as an extension of the building, and, compared with the previous example, the greater sophistication seems appropriate to its town situation, **4**. The protective concrete kerb is of some value but its projection would not be sufficient to save either cars or the wall from the effects of careless driving.

1.06 Total integration of building and surroundings obtained by continuity of material is seen at Harvey Court, Gonville and Caius, Cambridge, **5**; hard landscape indeed, but where warmth of colour from the brown bricks and a splendid use of geometric forms provide interest. The detailing of the low fascia has not been successful but the use of bull-nosed bricks softens the low wall top, while laying the coping bricks to a fall is practical as well as adding interest.

1.07 A typical old garden enclosure wall providing shelter and a background to planting is shown in **6** (unfortunately the value of colour cannot be illustrated here). Traditionally in subdued reds and browns, the basic colour is given some

4 Sophisticated town situation at the Tara Hotel, London.
5 Continuity of material with careful attention to brick detailing (Harvey Court, Gonville and Caius, Cambridge).
6 Deep red brick walling is a widely appreciated feature of many old gardens.
7 With this suburban garden wall at Ringsted, Denmark, the light coloured brickwork emphasises texture and provides strong contrast to selective planting.
8 Brick wall enclosures to a roof garden in Rome.

9

12a

10

12b

11a

12c

11b

12d

added interest by minor variations on and between the individual bricks while maintaining its overall low-key effect as a background to mixed planting. By contrast, the Danish garden boundary wall in **7** is more obviously designed as a feature in its own right with its mixture of textured and plain wall. The plain wall dramatises the shape of carefully selected planting and emphasises both the heavy modelling of the projecting bricks and the horizontal jointing throughout.

1.08 Another heavy-texture pattern wall is illustrated in **8**, this time enclosing an Italian roof garden. In this example the texture is again obtained by the arrangement of the bricks.

In **9** a less obtrusive texturing results from the use of hand-made bricks including a number which are deliberately 'misshapen' units.

In **10** overburnt lumps of clamp-fired brick material give an

appearance nearer to that of random stone than brick.

1.09 All of the above examples are of a texture which shows clearly at some distance. With plain brickwork the shape of joints and their colour contrast to the bricks has an important influence, both upon the apparent overall colour of a wall and upon the distance at which bond pattern becomes an effective feature of the design, **11, 12**.

9 *Rough textured brick used by Saarinen at Philadelphia University.*
10 *Lumps of overburnt clamp-fired material, useless for normal walling, provide a durable wall not unlike the*

effect of random stonework.
11, 12 *At close viewing subtle effects of brick shape and texture, and prominence and interest of bond pattern become significant.*

13 *Open screen wall links buildings and defines an upper level without obstructing the view (Aarhus University).*
14 *Another screen wall at Aarhus.*

2 Linking walls

2.01 Garden walls are sometimes used as linking features between buildings. Two interesting examples, **13** and **14**, are from Aarhus University, Denmark. In **13** the linking screen is an open design marking the edge of a high level courtyard. Figure **14** shows a combination of textured solid wall and access through arched brick columns combined with planting.

15 *A very simple pattern of brickwork giving some privacy without total enclosure.*
16 *to* **20** *Interesting open screen wall units at a*

brickworks in Kampala, Uganda, show possibilities for developments in manufacture.

3 Perforated walls

3.01 Perforated screen walls are useful in providing some shelter, either from wind or for privacy, while still allowing some view. With careful design of the size of openings they can act almost as one-way viewing barriers, vision depending upon distance from the screen—rather as with net curtains. In its simplest form, this may involve no more than a quarter or half brick space between units, as in **15**, where back yard screening is the objective. Design can vary from more elaborate patterns formed with ordinary bricks to very open types constructed from special units. The latter could be in most intricate shapes if more manufacturers would make examples comparable to those in **16** to **20**, which are displays of the products of a brickworks in Kampala, Uganda.

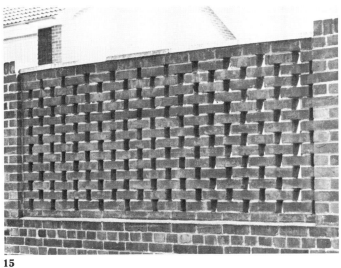
15

18

16

19

17

20

4 Freestanding walls

4.01 Freestanding walls can be subject to considerable lateral force from wind. Normally the wall thickness, alone or supplemented by piers at intervals, is relied upon but the requirement for lateral strength can be turned to advantage in other ways. In **21** a garden screen wall uses lateral buttress walls to form sheltered sitting alcoves, while **22** illustrates the famous Jefferson serpentine wall at the University of Virginia, a typical example of that eccentric's genius which has been widely copied because the shaping economically provides stability as well as interest.

21 Buttress projections to freestanding wall gives protection to seating (Hille Library, Harvard).

22 The famous serpentine garden wall at Charlottesville, US.

5 Retaining walls

5.01 Earth-retaining walls have particular technical problems (discussed later, page 70). Their appearance is usually governed by the same factors as other solid walls. An exception is the use of sloped surfaces to link two levels without an abrupt vertical face. An example of this treatment is shown in **24**, used in combination with a vertical earth-retaining wall and brick steps, all of which, in the same material, link the adjacent building to its immediate surroundings. Something of the same kind is achieved in a very informal way in the steps and 'rockery' wall shown in **23**, an architect's own house at Amersfoort, Holland.

23 Small scale and informal steps and planted sloping wall in an architect's garden at Amersfoort in Holland.

24 Sloping brickwork as an alternative to a vertical retaining wall (Lancaster University).

21

22

23

24

Malt Lane, Alcester: simple curved wall and radial paving increase the visual interest.

16

*Malt Lane, Alcester: the texture of brick paving has a
positive and unifying effect; cobbles protect planting.*

1 Exploiting the potential of brick paving

1.01 Although a great deal of brick paving is used effectively, there are examples where designers seem to fail because they have not fully appreciated the variety and potential of the material.

1.02 The large-scale urban area in The Netherlands shown in **1** is used by light wheeled traffic and pedestrians but not by a hurrying town crowd. There is an obvious need to provide as much interest as possible and the designer has used three methods. First, the large area is brought down in scale and given some overall interest by using three colours to divide the space. The squares are in brownish brick, the stripes in a darker tone of plum colour and the small squares at the strip inter-sections in blue-black. The second interest effect comes from the pattern of bricks in the squares which, although simple, is pleasing. The third effect is the result of the texture of bricks and joints, which is far from smooth, **2**. This texture, while contributing to the overall appearance, is probably most important as an interest factor to unhurried pedestrians.

1.03 Another example from The Netherlands, **3**, illustrates both pavements and roadway, providing attractive texture and

1 *Scale and interest of large area of paving affected by colour and pattern (Zetten-Andelst, The Netherlands).*
2 *Close-up of brick paving in **1** showing close viewing* *interest from type of brick and bond pattern.*
3 *If the Dutch can provide this kind of interest why is it not more often done elsewhere? (Amsterdam).*

1

3

2

4

6

7

9

5

8

a colour and scale that is in harmony with the buildings. Example **4** shows that material needs to be carefully chosen and sensitively used: the rather smooth surfaced pavers suffer from an absence of imaginative design. It also highlights the importance of appreciating total effect. Presumably intended to look flat, the arrangement of falls to achieve drainage results in an up-and-down appearance, which is irritatingly obtrusive, particularly because of the smoothness and even shape of the units and their severe bonding pattern. By contrast, the meticulous workmanship combined with regular shaped smooth pavers in a small and busy pedestrian urban situation, **5**, is most attractive. Note that in this example the pavers are laid with their long sides at right angles to the line of traffic and therefore the maximum advantage of joints as non-slip aids is obtained for the smooth-surfaced units.

1.04 In a different situation, **6**, smooth and regular shaped pavers would not be suitable; the rougher appearance with its

almost casual edging is appropriate for strolling through the park. Another example of sympathetic choice and use of material is shown in **7** where paving is closely related to an adjacent building. At a grander level, more decorative treatment may seem appropriate as in the open-jointed fan pattern of brickwork in a covered way at Rhenen, The Netherlands, **8**.

2 Brick used with other materials

2.01 A mixture of materials is acceptable. In **9** a large forecourt area is reduced in scale and given added interest by a formal pattern of contrasting colours. In this case there is also functional use of the lighter colour to mark the edges of steps. At St James Square, Grimsby, **10**, and at High Street, Lincoln, **11**, brick paving is used to break the large area of concrete slabs and to mark a frequently used pedestrian route.

10

11

12

4 A large area of smooth-faced brick pavers where the possibilities of the material have not been used to advantage (high level walkway, Barbican, London).
5 A busy pedestrian route in down-town San Francisco. Smooth surface bricks used

well (the promenade, San Francisco).
6 Informality is the key to the attraction of this garden path (Monterey, California).
7 Small scale situation with paving to match the nearby walls (library at Great Missenden, Bucks).

8 Imaginative treatment for paving using open jointing (Rhenen, The Netherlands).
9 Bricks and concrete provide colour contrast for large scale pattern (The Hilles Library, Harvard, US).
10 Brickwork used to indicate a pedestrian route across a

paved square (St James Square, Grimsby).
11 A more haphazard mixture of brick and concrete (High Street, Lincoln).
12 Brick and stone and planting are the ingredients for this restful backwater (Bunhill Fields).

14

15

2.02 Mixed materials, stone and brick, are used in a bold but simple arrangement at Trinity College, Oxford, with the brick joints gravel filled **14**. Again, at Bunhill Fields, **12**, brick and stone are both used, while example **13** shows that a happy mixture of materials is also possible in small-scale situations.
2.03 The comfortable and friendly appearance of brickwork is used to good effect in parts of the Marquess Road Housing Estate in London. A scale and colour relationship between the buildings and the paving provides a robust and interesting finish, **15**.
2.04 Note joints running across the direction of traffic and the suitability of the fairly rough texture for providing safety on slopes as well as on flat paths. Another housing estate with similar treatment is Lillington Street, Westminster, **16**. The brick edge provides a good stop for the grass, without obstruction to a mower. The upstand edge may also be sufficient to discourage at least some spoiling of grass edges.

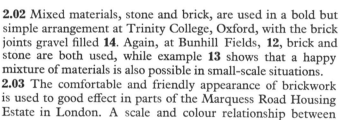

13 *Mixed materials can also be interesting in small-scale intimate situations (Tuin Staffen, The Netherlands).*
14 *A mixture of brick and stone, with brick joints filled with small gravel (Trinity College, Oxford).*
15 *Walls and paving in matching bricks (Marquess Road housing, Islington).*
16 *The upstand edge provides some protection to the grass. Mowing is no problem (Lillington Street, Westminster).*

16

17

18

19

3 Brick plinths

3.01 The careful design of transition from building walls to adjacent ground is apparent in many recent buildings. Sometimes a complete matching of the material is obtained; an example of this, with the link carried through as large radiused brick coving, is illustrated in Chapter 1, **7**.

3.02 In **17** a sloping plinth is a major design feature, carefully detailed to appear as an integral part of the building and with its brown brickwork continued for the paving. In **18** the paving and sloping plinth (all in pavers) form a base, emphasised by a horizontal projection from the building walls and by differences in colour and size between pavers and walling bricks. In **19**, with plinth and wall of similar material, the junction of grass and sloping brickwork may prove awkward for mowing and might have looked more effective with at least a narrow strip of flat paving at ground level.

4 Brick roads

4.01 In Britain, unfortunately, brick paving is largely confined to areas of pedestrian usage. In other countries, and especially in The Netherlands, its aesthetic appeal is more appreciated.

4.02 Three Dutch examples, **21 a, b, c** show its use for roads and car parking, but **22**, the famous Lombard Street in San Francisco, is perhaps the most spectacular example of a brick road.

20

17 *The building to ground link is by means of a sloping plinth which is a major feature of the design (Target House, Aylesbury).*
18 *Paths and plinth in clay pavers differ in colour from the red brick building (John Dalton College, Manchester).*
19 *The plinth to ground junction may cause mowing problems (library at Maidenhead).*
20 *Laid on a suitable base, perforated bricks provide instant drainage without laying to falls and are suitable for parking area usage.*
21 a, b, c *Three examples of Dutch roads and parking areas.*
22 *Perhaps the most famous brick-paved road in the world,*

Lombard Street, San Francisco. A great tourist sight as well as a background for cops and robbers in fast cars.

23

21a

21b

21c

22

*Brick pavements and roads in the Hanover city centre
redevelopment: the road bond pattern laid diagonally in the
traditional manner reduces risk of displacement by vehicles.*

Chapter 4: Miscellaneous landscape features

1 Introduction

1.01 The examples discussed so far have illustrated general walling and paving and have shown how, by taking advantage of the potentialities of the material, brickwork can provide a wide variety of colour, scale and texture for situations varying from an urban street to a rural garden. Whatever the situation the basic design will often need to incorporate features such as steps, surrounds, sculptures and play spaces, or perhaps something added purely for visual interest. In all cases these features must fit happily into the overall design.

2 Brick steps

2.01 The first example, **1**, shows simple brick paving using bricks laid on the flat but with step edges formed with bricks on edge. This has the advantage of marking step edges and thereby adding to safety. In **2** where hotel steps meet a sloping pavement of similar material, there is no emphasis at the edge of the steps. In the photograph, taken in strong sunlight, the risers appear to show up quite clearly, but at night this would occur only with carefully directed lighting. In **3** and **4** extra emphasis is given by the shadow on the recessed lower part of the riser. Note the generous dimension of the treads in **3**.

1 *Brick pattern helps to mark the step edges (flats at Avenue Road, London NW8).*
2 *Hotel steps. With the difficult problem of levels a* *clearer definition of risers would have been helpful (Hyatt Hotel, San Francisco).*
3 *The overhang of paver treads gives a shadow line* *which helps to mark the risers as well as adding visual interest.*
4 *Stepped platforms combined with water* *(Blackwell's Scientific Publications, Oxford).*

5

7

8a

8b

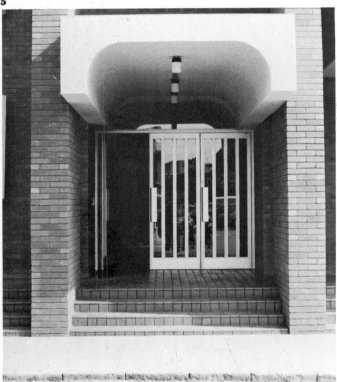

6

8c

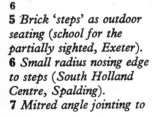

5 *Brick 'steps' as outdoor seating (school for the partially sighted, Exeter).*
6 *Small radius nosing edge to steps (South Holland Centre, Spalding).*
7 *Mitred angle jointing to* steps *(South Downs College, Havant).*
8a, b, c *A more relaxed approach, treating the steps as very incidental features in the landscape (Graham Park, Hendon).*

case, the steps are close to a cleanly detailed building, the carefully mitred corners maintain a continuity of character.
2.04 Normally a hard brick provides adequate resistance to damage but for hard wear situations a rounded edge 'nosing' is an extra safeguard. For comfort and safety the nosing should be kept to a small radius, as in **6**, although in this particular example the safety aspect may have been compromised by the reduced rise of the lowest step. (On sloping sites there is inevitably a problem, but insufficient attention to the importance of keeping equal risers is quite frequently apparent at entrances to buildings even on flat sites.)
2.05 An alternative to the more formal examples shown above is to treat steps not so much as an interruption to the landscape but as a casual feature of it, **8**, with simple brick on edge nosings and shallow risers.

2.02 In outdoor situations, where space restriction is not a major factor, it is often appropriate to use a relatively small rise with a large tread. Deep treads can also have other uses, **5**.
2.03 Where steps include returns, careful detailing can have a considerable effect on appearance. The example in **4** might be inappropriate in a rustic situation, but where, as in this

3 Tree surrounds

3.01 Trees located in paved areas interrupt the paving. This provides an opportunity to form a design feature in the paving. The design should always allow for growth of the tree (with an increase in the size of the trunk) and for adequate water supply to the roots. In addition, especially for young trees, protection against damage may be needed.

3.02 A simple design is shown in **9** in which rectangular cast iron drainage grids have been carefully sized to fit into brick paving without any cutting.

9 *Rectangular cast iron tree grids co-ordinated with paving unit sizes (town square, Bracknell).*

10

10 *Integrated design of paving, seating and tree location (General Hospital, Southampton).*

11

11 *Tree positions used as basis for interesting paving pattern (King's Lynn).*

3.03 In **10**, trees, seating and the paving pattern form part of a comprehensive treatment which adds interest to the scene in a fairly simple way. The octagonal design involves care in setting out and an appreciable amount of simple cutting of the pavers.

3.04 In **11**, maximum advantage is taken of the adaptability of the small size of paving unit to provide interesting patterns. Fairly elaborate patterning of this kind looks particularly good when seen from above. With unjointed rings of brick around the trees there is good access for rain penetration and as the tree grows, inner rings of paving can be readily removed. A more straightforward arrangement is shown in **12**, but the effect has been spoilt by the surrounding paving.

12 This could have been as interesting as 11, but is let down by its surroundings (Graham Park, Hendon).

12

13

4 Unwanted features

4.01 In town paving a wide variety of tiresome objects such as lamp posts, signposts, and access covers to gas, water, electricity and telephones, usually occur. Unless these can all be finally positioned before the paving is laid, a great deal of extra labour is involved in coming back to make good and, all too often, the final result is unsatisfactory. On almost all jobs, however, the commonest 'interruption' to paving tends to be drainage manhole covers. These are normally within the control of the general designer but, unless their location is most carefully considered and their precise positioning is ensured by good site supervision, there will be some very irritating results. Photograph **14** shows manhole covers which are carefully arranged to give the least possible offence, whereas, from the same job, **13** shows a cover which intrudes across two materials and has involved almost the maximum amount of cutting to the large concrete slabs.

13 Manhole position is visually unfortunate and also involves considerable cutting of the paving (school at Exeter).
14 Careful location of manholes (school for the partially sighted, Exeter).

14

15

16

17

4.02 Neat and careful use of the manhole cover is shown in **15**, with two bad examples in **16** and **17**.

15 Carefully integrated manhole cover with brick infill (Preston).
16 An attractive mixture of brick and concrete paving marred by the unfortunate

placing of the manhole cover (High Street, Lincoln).
17 Unsightly covers actually raised above paving level (Barbican, London).

18

5 Planting containers

5.01 It is often best to keep the design of plant containers as simple as possible, to avoid fussy competition with the plants themselves. Only standard bricks are used in the examples in **18** to **20**. The very simple marking of the planted areas, **18**, defines them unobtrusively but by raising the plants slightly above the paving adds interest through enabling the vegetation to grow down to the paving level. In **19**, too, the 'construction' is simple, relying upon basic shapes rather than fussy details. In **20** the curved and stepped walls take advantage of the site conditions, but again the construction is kept simple so that, when fully grown, the planting will provide the detailed interest.

5.02 A totally different design approach is evident in **21**, where the brickwork is treated as an extension to the nearby building, with meticulous workmanship and special shaped brick units.

18 Very simple containment of planting near ground level (The Netherlands).
19a, b Two views of simple brick containers for water planting (Amersfoort, The Netherlands).
20 Curved and stepped walls make good use of site

conditions. Brickwork is kept simple (garden in The Netherlands).
21 More elaborate design with careful workmanship in planting boxes which relate to nearby building (Commonwealth War Graves Commission, Maidenhead).

19a

19b

20

21

22

22 *Circular fountain at the Tower Hotel, London.*

23 *Circular fountains at the Maidenhead Library,* **a**, *and*

at Queen Elizabeth Close, Norwich, **b**.

6 Circular features

6.01 Photographs **22** to **25** show further uses of brickwork in circular designs. Two-way curves in standard units are used in the brick faced elephant wall at the London Zoo, **24**, and in a neat equipment enclosure (which is really more a brick feature in the landscape than a building) in **25**.

6.02 A transition from large concrete slab paving to brickwork for the circular surround to a pool at Maidenhead Library is illustrated in **23a**, with a simple 'special' brick shape used for the junction from sloping sides to flat top.

6.03 At the Tower Hotel, London, **22**, the paving surrounding the circular fountain is also brick, as are the embankment walls and enclosures.

24 *Two-way curves in standard bricks (London Zoo).*
25 *A very neat piece of street furniture with curves in two directions (LEB generator, Chelsea Embankment, London).*

24

25

26

7 Sculpture

7.01 In previous chapters examples were shown of decorative walling, with varying degrees of scale and pattern obtained by the arrangement of the brick units. The material can also be used in a variety of ways for sculpture.

7.02 Photograph **26** shows normal bricks used to form a freestanding feature in a shopping area in Chandler's Ford,

26 *Normal bricklaying used in freestanding sculptural feature (shopping centre at Chandler's Ford, Hants).*

27

28

29b

29c

29a

30

while **27** reveals a different application inside a building combining fairly simple cutting with normal brickwork. The more usual sculptural techniques of carving are also frequently used. Incised designs can be carried out by sandblasting, **28**, while **29** illustrates chiselling for a relief work by Henry Moore at the Bouwcentrum in Rotterdam. This was originally intended for bronze but was eventually executed by two master masons working from a plaster model.

7.03 In the past, wealthy landowners sometimes designed garden follies, which presumably fall into the periphery of 'hard landscape'. The tower in the campus of Dallas University, **30**, which is quite a feature in the local landscape, might be regarded as a modern equivalent.

27 Wall sculpture formed by reasonably simple cutting of bricks (technical school, Deventer, The Netherlands).
28 Blast carved brickwork: Canterbury Tales (New central library, Grays, Essex. Copyright: William Mitchell Design Consultants Ltd).
29 Designed by Henry Moore, originally for bronze, this brick sculpture was carved

by masons (Bouwcentrum, Rotterdam).
30 A brick feature in the campus at Dallas University. A latter-day folly?

31a

31a-d *Decorative use of brick on a minaret at Gulpaygan, Iran (circa* 1100).

7.04 Meanwhile towers of many kinds form important features in the landscape, eg bell towers, water towers. The 900-year old minaret from Persia (**31a-d**) is a typical example of the highly decorative possibilities of brick construction used in Seljuk architecture.

31b

31c

31d

8 Play areas

8.01 Delightful shapes can be produced in brick for adventurous play by children, as Michael Brown's playground in Paddington, London, shows, **32, 33**. A less exuberant, but much enjoyed, space is on the GLC estate at Hendon, **34**.

32, 33 *A bit of fun for the children (Brunel Estate, Paddington, London).*
34 *Rather more sober enjoyment (Graham Park, Hendon).*

32

33

34

38

35 This photograph of brick landscaping at Sunderland sums up the possibilities of brick as a paving material. Steps and ramps in straight bonded rectangular units, and general paving, jointly provide extra interest from the different shape of pavers. It must also be great fun for children on roller skates.

Part 2: The material

Chapter 5: Selection of bricks

1 Introduction

1.01 The widespread and longstanding use of brickwork has ensured a good understanding of the general properties of the material. Much that applies to ordinary building work is also relevant to brickwork used in hard landscape. A major difference is that landscape brickwork is subject to greater exposure and wetting leaving it more vulnerable to frost. Particular aspects of design and the correct use of materials for paving, freestanding walls and earth-retaining walls are given later, but to avoid unnecessary repetition information which applies generally is given here.

2 Specification

British Standards

2.01 The three key Standards for brickwork are:
BS 3921:1974 *Specification for clay bricks and blocks.* This refers to standard metric units and covers standard size and quality requirements.
BS 187: Part 2: 1970 *Specification for calcium silicate (sandlime and flintlime) bricks.* This refers to standard metric units and covers shape and quality. It also includes recommendations for mortar mixes for differing situations.
BS 4729:1971 *Metric and imperial units. Specification for shapes and dimensions of special bricks.* Note that the term 'special bricks' as used in BS 4729 refers only to shape. The term 'special' is also commonly used in relation to quality, eg in BS 3921. There are no British Standards concerned only with bricks used as pavers.

Brick size

2.02 The Standards refer to 'work size' which is the actual size of the unit, **1a**, subject to specified tolerances. The brick-plus-joint dimensions are now generally referred to as 'format', **1b**. The BS format is 225 × 112·5 × 75 mm. A number of manufacturers also make 'modular' sized bricks. The format sizes of these include: 300 × 100 × 100 mm; 300 × 100 × 75 mm; 200 × 100 × 100 and 200 × 100 × 75 mm.

Brick paver sizes

2.03 While standard or modular bricks are frequently used for paving, 'pavers' are also made specifically for this purpose. There is no BS to cover these. Pavers are thinner than standard bricks but may also vary considerably in their other dimensions. Information on paver sizes is given in table I, page 43.

Special shaped bricks

2.04 BS 4729 illustrates a considerable number of shapes, all to suit the BS format. These shapes, most of which are fairly readily available, are generally referred to as 'standard specials'. Other shapes, which may be made to order, are often referred to as 'specials' or 'special specials'. Some examples of shaped bricks commonly used in landscape brickwork are referred to later, but the following general points should be noted:

● If not available from stock a considerable time may be needed for manufacture and delivery.

● It is important to foresee all requirements, eg if a double bullnosed brick is used as a coping extra shapes would be needed to form the internal and external angles and also at wall ends, **2**.

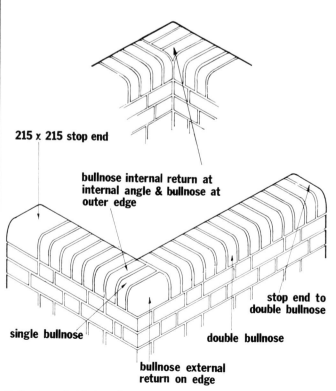

215 x 215 stop end

bullnose internal return at internal angle & bullnose at outer edge

stop end to double bullnose

single bullnose

double bullnose

bullnose external return on edge

2 Bullnose brick on edge coping.

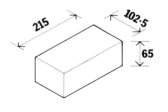

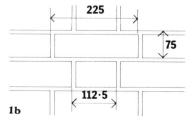

215   102·5   65   225   75   112·5

1a   **1b**

1 BS brick sizes: **a** *work size;* **b** *format.*

● Special manufacture of small quantities inevitably increases cost. 'Special specials' should not be included if 'standard specials' could provide a substantially similar result. It appears that designers not infrequently call for specially made units without first exploring the possibilities of more readily available shapes.

● With clay bricks, special shapes might mean that differences in manufacture, particularly in firing, could result in slightly different colours from the standard bricks. Some manufacturers will, if given enough notice, fire standard brick and specials together to eliminate the possibility.

● Unusual shapes or a requirement for bricks larger than normal size may present manufacturing problems.

2.05 For all the above reasons it is essential that early consideration should be given to the full range of requirements so that when the standard bricks are chosen any problem about specials can also be dealt with. Direct consultation with the brick manufacturer may be very helpful, both in confirming what specials are available from stock and in ensuring that 'special specials' are feasible in design, can be produced when required and will maintain continuity in appearance.

Perforated bricks

2.06 In recent years there has been a considerable increase in the use of perforated bricks. There is no evidence to suggest that these when correctly used are any less durable than solid bricks of similar manufacture. During construction the perforations allow rain penetration to occur more readily, and while protection against rain penetration through the tops of walls during construction should be regarded as essential good practice for any brickwork, it is especially important with perforated bricks.

3 Brick durability

Calcium silicate bricks

3.01 BS requirements for durability in severe exposure conditions differ for calcium silicate and clay bricks. In BS 187 calcium silicate bricks are graded in eight classes, with strength as the main determining factor, table I. For freestand-ing walls, bricks should be class 3 or higher. For copings and for earth-retaining walls, class 4 or higher should be chosen. The BS does not refer to the choice of calcium silicate bricks for paving, but it is reasonable to assume that class 4 or higher would have adequate frost resistance.

Clay bricks

3.02 BS 3921 for clay bricks describes three classes:
1 for internal walls;
2 facing and common bricks of ordinary quality;
3 facing and common bricks of special quality.

3.03 The BS also classifies clay brick into eight grades for 'loadbearing brick' plus two grades, A and B, for 'engineering brick'. The loadbearing grades are determined by strength only. The engineering grades are determined by strength and absorption. While a grade A engineering and, almost always, a grade B engineering brick will be frost resistant under conditions of severe exposure, there is no satisfactory laboratory test to determine frost resistance of the other eight strength grades. There is ample evidence that some clay bricks of low strength and relatively high absorption are very durable and entirely suitable for use in high exposure situations. The BS therefore suggests that evidence of adequate performance over a period of three years' exposure is the best guide. Where this evidence is not obtainable, special quality bricks should have either a minimum strength of $48 \cdot 5$ N/mm² or a water absorption not greater than 7 per cent.

3.04 It is therefore recommended that for earth-retaining walls, copings and paving, bricks should comply with the special quality requirements for soluble salts content and, whenever possible, should be checked for frost resistance by evidence of performance under conditions of exposure and of design details similar to the intended usage.

3.05 For the general area of brickwork in freestanding walls it is even more difficult to make precise recommendations. Many ordinary quality facing bricks are satisfactory in many situations, and to impose special quality requirements could unnecessarily limit choice and increase costs. To take manufacturers' advice or evidence from built examples seems to be the only sensible course to adopt.

Table I Physical and mechanical requirements of calcium silicate bricks
(Table II BS 187: Part 2: 1970)

Physical or mechanical requirement	Appendix	Class of brick							
		7	5	4	3A	3B	2A	2B	1
Compressive strength (wet): average of ten bricks in MN/m² to be not less than:	B	48·5	34·5	27·5	20·5	20·5	14·0	14·0	7·0
Uniformity of compressive strength: coefficient of variation in % not to exceed:	C	16	16	20	20	20	30	30	30
Drying shrinkage: % of original wet length measurement not to exceed:	D	0·025	0·025	0·025	0·025	0·035	0·025	0·035	—

Note: drying shrinkage of bricks used under permanently damp conditions is of no significance and the test for bricks to be used under these conditions is therefore unnecessary.

4

3,4 *Bodnant Garden in Gwynedd, North Wales (National Trust): old paving laid around 1875, in which the patterns add interest. The edge treatment allows spreading plants to protrude without breaking into the main patterned area.*

Chapter 6: External paving: sizes of bricks; their effect on laying patterns

1 Paving materials

Type of material

1.01 Clay units have been used for external paving for centuries. More recently calcium silicate bricks have also been used.

Unit size

1.02 Either BS standard or metric modular bricks may be used exposing their normal face. Some, particularly clay bricks made by the wire-cut process, are also suitable for use in the 'on-flat' position. Special clay pavers, in a more limited range of colours, are also available. There is considerable variation between manufacturers in the sizes of pavers. Thicknesses may vary between 20 and 65 mm. Exposed face size of pavers is often the BS work size of 215 × 102·5 mm but other shapes are also made (table I).

1.03 With evenly bedded units, laid on a good base, thickness has little practical effect upon performance. Thin units have the advantage of lower unit cost and lower transport cost and perhaps rather easier handling when laying.

1.04 Basic cost of the units should be assessed in terms of area rather than price per thousand. Table I shows the number of units per square metre for a variety of sizes when joints are 10 mm wide.

Strength

2.02 The average compressive strengths of units range from about 7 to 100 N/mm². Table II shows the strengths of various classes as defined in British Standards.

2.03 Resistance to cracking under load or impact depends more upon the quality of base and even bedding than upon inherent strength of the units. There does not appear to be any authoritative guidance relating unit strength requirement to type of traffic but the fact that most clay pavers fall within the engineering classes may be an indication that fairly high strength is needed if a wide range of conditions is to be met. It is worth noting that the passage of an occasional heavy vehicle, eg a service truck or fire engine, could cause unexpected damage over an area designed solely with pedestrian use in mind.

Often mechanical damage is more evident as spoiling of arrises than breaking of units. The incidence of such damage depends upon strength of units and upon joint design and is more noticeable where units are very regular in shape. Flush finished mortar joints protect the arrises but for moderately heavy traffic a tough brick with recessed joints can be satisfactory. A compromise is a slightly dished joint. Some clay pavers are made with bevelled edges which are resistant to damage.

2.04 Calcium silicate bricks are usually regular in shape and vulnerable to arris damage unless flush jointed.

Table I Commonly available sizes of bricks and pavers. Number of units per square metre of paving allowing for 10 mm joints. No allowance for cutting or waste

Type	Unit work size (mm)	Exposed face format (mm)		No per m²	M² per 1000
BS bricks	215 × 102·5 × 65	On edge	225 × 75;	60	16·66
		on flat	225 × 112·5	40	25·00
Metric modular bricks	290 × 90 × 90		300 × 100	33	30·30
	290 × 90 × 65	On edge	300 × 75;	44	32·73
		on flat	300 × 100	33	30·30
	190 × 90 × 90		200 × 100	50	20·00
	190 × 90 × 65	On edge	200 × 75;	66	15·15
		on flat	200 × 100	50	20·00
Pavers	215 × 102·5 × 20, 33, 40, 50, 55, 60		225 × 112·5	40	25·00
	215 × 65 × 33		225 × 75	60	16·66
	215 × 140 × 33		225 × 150	30	33·33
	190 × 90 × 50		200 × 100	50	20·00
	250 × 125 × 50		260 × 135	28	35·71
	300 × 150 × 50		310 × 160	20	50·00

Table II Brick strength as defined in British Standards 187 and 3921

Type	Minimum average compressive strength N/mm²
Clay engineering class A	69·0
Clay engineering class B	48·5
Clay loadbearing from class 1 to class 15	7·0 103·5
Calcium silicate* from class 4 to class 7	27·5 48·5

* Calcium silicate classes 1 to 3 not shown as not recommended for external paving.

2 Properties of materials

Resistances to exposure

2.01 General aspects of ²te requirements for durability were considered in Chapter 5. For paving the following recommendations are made: calcium silicate bricks should be to BS 187 class 4 or higher; clay bricks and pavers should meet the requirements for bricks of special quality as defined in BS 3921.

Safety

2.05 Many ordinary facing bricks have a surface texture which provides a good non-slip finish. Dense material (generally the high strength bricks and pavers) has a very smooth surface which is inclined to be rather slippery. Some hard pavers, especially those made by the wire-cut process, have a surface texture which adds to safety. Some hard type bricks are made with a dimpled or chequered pattern.

2.06 The frequent joints in brick paving considerably help to provide a good grip. Maximum benefit of jointing is obtained when main joint lines run across the direction of traffic, **1**.

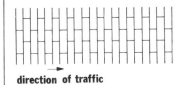

direction of traffic

1 *Slipperiness is reduced by running joint lines across the direction of traffic.*

It is worth taking advantage of this when detailing ramps. While there is little complaint about slipperiness of external brick paving in towns, the growth of moss or lichen can sometimes be troublesome on smooth units elsewhere. This is most likely to occur in rural areas and under trees or on shaded areas close to the north side of buildings. For such areas the use of textured brick and recessed joints is advised.

3 Bond patterns

3.01 Joint pattern plays a significant part in the appearance of any brickwork. In walling there are practical aspects which limit the possibilities. The absence of many of these restraints permits far more flexibility in paving—a fact that does not seem to be exploited as often as it might be. In determining patterns the following general points might be considered:
● does the chosen unit face size give the scale required or should a second scale be superimposed, **2**?
● will a proposed pattern involve special units or an unacceptable amount of cutting? Note that edge cutting becomes relatively less important as areas increase, **3**;
● is a directional pattern required:
1 to emphasise a particular route;
2 to provide maximum joint grip, **1** (para 2.06);
3 to improve water run-off from minimum fall areas, **4**?
● is a good interlocking pattern required to prevent lateral displacement? It seems significant that in The Netherlands, where brick paved roads are common, the units are frequently laid in herringbone pattern, **5**;
● is advantage taken of the considerable differences in appearance that result from units of different exposed face size or shape being used for basically similar patterns, **6**?
3.02 With more complex patterns the variation in effect can be very apparent, **7**.
3.03 It will be found that the 300 × 100 × 75 mm and 200 × 100 × 75 mm modular sizes, with the 75 mm dimension exposed, are not suitable for some arrangements commonly used with standard bricks.
3.04 Some other commonly used basic patterns are shown in 3:1 and 2:1 face proportions. To avoid a multiplicity of diagrams the examples are restricted mostly to units having the same longest dimensions, **8**, **10**.

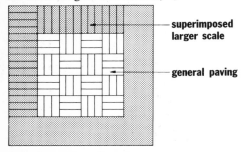

2 *Scale can be adjusted considerably by incorporating a second colour.*

superimposed larger scale

general paving

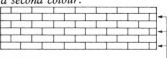

cutting / specials required

3 *It is necessary to cut some bricks in most paving layouts. The cutting becomes*

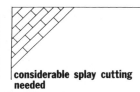

considerable splay cutting needed

less obtrusive as area increases, and when simpler patterns are used.

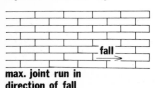

max. joint run in direction of fall

fall

4 *Where falls are shallow, run-off is improved if predominant joints run in the direction of the fall.*

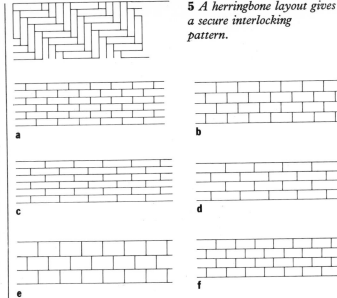

5 *A herringbone layout gives a secure interlocking pattern.*

6a *Standard brick on edge, 225 × 75 mm format;* **b** *standard brick on flat, 225 × 112·5 mm format;* **c** *large metric modular on edge, 300 × 75 mm format;* **d** *large metric modular on* flat, 300 × 100 mm format; **e** *wide pavers, 225 × 150 mm format;* **f** *small metric modular on flat, 200 × 100 mm format.*

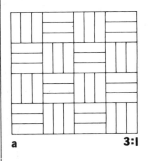

a   3:1

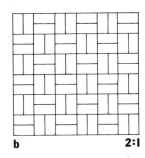

b   2:1

7 *Basket weave:* **a** *3:1 proportion on face;* **b** *2:1 proportion on face.*

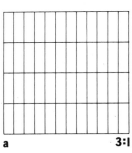

a   3:1

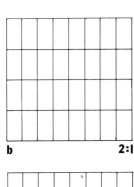

b   2:1

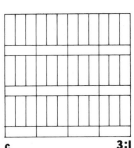

c   3:1

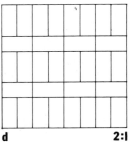

d   2:1

8a, b *Stack bond;* **c, d** *stack bond and running bond mixed.*

9 *Circular pattern in the crypt of a church in Collevalenze.*

9→

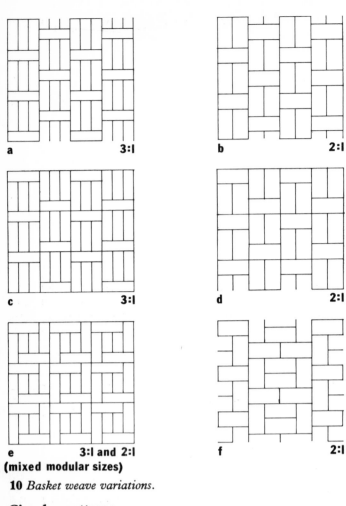

10 *Basket weave variations.*

Circular patterns

3.05 Although special shaped units could be used it is common practice to form circular patterns from rectangular units. With a small radius pattern the outer ends of wedge-shaped joints can look unpleasant if they become very wide, **11**. Four examples are given as an indication. They are all of standard bricks and each case assumes a minimum joint width of 7 mm, **12**.

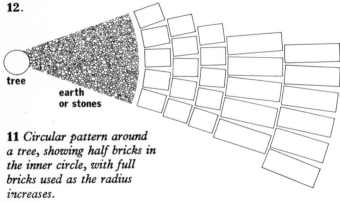

11 *Circular pattern around a tree, showing half bricks in the inner circle, with full bricks used as the radius increases.*

Method of calculating the splay dimensions in circular paving layouts, when brick size and radius are known, and gap between bricks on inner circumference is determined:

Formula		Worked example 10a[1]
$\dfrac{\text{inner circumference } (2\pi r)}{\text{inner module (brick width + space)}}$	= number of modules to circle	$\dfrac{6284}{65+7} = 87\cdot27$ modules[2]
then, $\dfrac{\text{outer circumference}}{\text{number of modules to circle}}$	= dimension of module at outer circle	$\dfrac{7635}{87\cdot27} = 87\cdot48$ mm
therefore, gap at outer edge	= dimension of outer module less brick width	$87\cdot48 - 65 = 22\cdot48$ mm

Note 1 In 10a, inner radius: 1000 mm; brick size: 65 × 215; inner gap: 7 mm.
    2 Not suitable, of course, if a complete circle pattern is required. The gap must (theoretically) be 7·229 mm to give 87 complete modules.

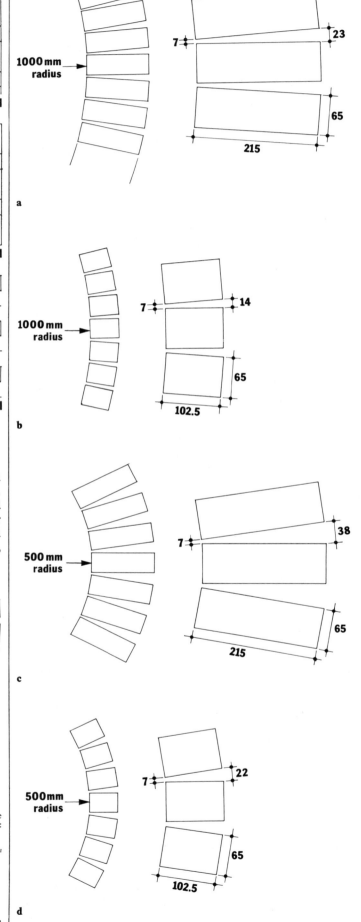

12 *The effect of radius and brick format on the success of circular patterns.*

Chapter 7: External paving

1 Surface drainage

Problems of falls

1.01 It is commonly recommended that external paving should be laid to falls of from 1:40 to 1:60, but, in replies to a questionnaire, some architects said they specified falls as little as 1:120. For small areas the total fall may not cause problems, but over large areas the effect upon both appearance and cost could be considerable. In determining falls the following aspects should be considered.

How essential is quick and total clearance of surface water?
1.02 For heavily used areas, either for vehicles or pedestrians, a fairly quick run-off is desirable, but perhaps more important is the need to avoid puddles. On areas adjacent to building entrances good clearance is needed. In parks or private gardens quick clearance may not be particularly necessary but enduring puddles should be prevented.

Is any fall necessary?
1.03 With some methods of construction, eg bedding and jointing with sand above a hardcore base, surface water quickly penetrates regardless of falls.

The effect of jointing method
1.04 Mortared joints largely prevent surface water dispersal by penetration. Recessed mortar joints and, to some extent, absorbent bricks, may help to prevent minor puddles.

Will specified falls be achieved?
1.05 A 1:60 fall is approximately 16 mm/m. How accurate is workmanship likely to be? Where good clearance is essential specifications should include a limit to local deviation from the overall fall, eg levels over any 2 m length should not deviate from the general fall lines by more than plus or minus, say, 8 mm. (The actual deviation figure should be related to the specified fall. With very slight overall falls very little latitude can be allowed.)

Will levels remain unchanged?
1.06 This depends primarily upon the type of base. A properly designed concrete base should ensure against uneven settlement. Other foundations are unlikely to do so and are therefore better avoided where accurate finishes are important. Settlement at the perimeter of paved areas should be prevented.

Will falls cause hazards?
1.07 The degree of fall, within the range required solely for water clearance, will not affect safe walking but could affect wheel chairs, shopping trolleys, or prams left without brakes on. Design should ensure that 'runaway' situations are avoided.

1 *Two-way run-off to adjacent ground.*

2 *Run-off to planting in preference to grass.*

Appearance

1.08 On small areas the falls needed for drainage seldom have any appreciable effect on appearance. On large areas, 'up and down' falls can be quite obtrusive. This is probably most noticeable when drainage is by two-way falls to point outlets, **8**.

Cost

1.09 On large areas there may be a cost advantage if paving can make use of natural ground falls. This may save on excavation or fill and may also help to reduce the need for tiresome or costly steps.

Recommendations on falls

For permeable paving
1.10 For drainage requirements falls are usually unnecessary. If this type of construction is used adjacent to buildings local falls away from doorways may be desirable.

For impermeable paving
1.11 In public areas where quick clearance and freedom from puddling is important (ie most urban situations and near any doorways) falls should be in the range of 1:40 to 1:60 with a specification limit on tolerances. Precautions for wheeled traffic may be needed.

For impermeable paving in casual use areas
1.12 In gardens and parks, falls of 1:60 to 1:120 are acceptable, depending upon importance of situation, frequency of drainage outlets and type of bricks and joints.

Arrangement of falls and outlets

1.13 Except where permeable construction makes falls unnecessary, there is a choice of four main systems. In the following diagrams, **1** to **8**, details of construction are not shown.

Run-off to adjacent ground

1.14 The system is shown in **1** and **2**.

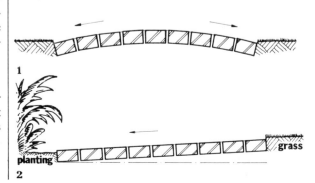

1

planting

2

grass

Advantage: no cost for outlets or drains, **1**.
Disadvantage: suitable only for small areas of paving and where adjacent ground will not suffer.
Use: where there is a choice, run-off to planted area rather than to grass, **2**.

Straight falls to open channels

1.15 This system is rather more hazardous than the others; it is illustrated in **3** to **7**.
Advantages: on moderate sized areas open channels may remove all water to gulleys at the perimeter, thus avoiding drains beneath the paving, **3**; on large areas if subsoil is able to take disposal into soakaways beneath the paving, open channels again avoid drains beneath paving, **4**.
Disadvantages: unless very carefully designed, an open channel may be a hazard to pedestrians.
Use: avoid in busy pedestrian areas. Where possible, avoid open channels running across line of traffic, **5**.
Design: channels need some fall towards outlets, say 1:60. If the perimeter of the whole paving is level, the channel falls mean variation in depth of channel which increases the obstruction hazard and complicates the construction, **6**.
If, in addition to the falls towards the channel, the whole area of paving can slope in the direction of the channels, the channels can be maintained at a constant depth, **7**.

Straight falls to covered channels with continuous drainage openings

1.16 Drainage openings may be slotted channel units or perforated or open jointed bricks over a channel or a metal grating. This is basically the same as method 1.15 but avoids the hazard of the open channel. Slotted types might still be a hazard to pedestrians with stiletto heeled shoes or perhaps to pram wheels.

Cross falls to point outlets

1.17 Safer than 1.15, this method may be visually less acceptable, **8**.
Advantage: avoids construction of channels and hazard of open channels.
Disadvantages: on large areas appearance may be less acceptable than systems 1.15 or 1.16. This is most likely to apply where paving is in smooth faced or regular shaped units. Diagonal junctions are more difficult to form and may entail cutting.
Use: perimeter of each drained area needs to be at constant level unless actual falls are increased to override the site fall. Note that the determined minimum fall should be on line ag and not bg, **8**.

Spacing of channels and gulleys

1.18 In terms of drainage requirements alone, it is not feasible to make precise recommendations for length of paving runs to channels or gulleys. Rain will obviously clear more quickly with steeper falls and with smooth rather than rough surfacing. In practice, on large areas where movement joints are needed it is sensible for these to coincide with positions where falls divide, so spacing and joints need to be considered together.

Movement joints

1.19 Where paving is mortar bedded and jointed, movement joints are recommended. Again, there is little reliable information about exact requirements. On theoretical grounds it seems reasonable to locate movement joints at not more than 10 m intervals. Joints in the paving should coincide with all joints in any concrete base, so in practice this will usually be the governing factor.*

---

* For details of base concrete joints, including dowel jointing between bays to obviate differential vertical movement, see Gage, M., and Vandenberg, M., *Hard Landscape in Concrete*.

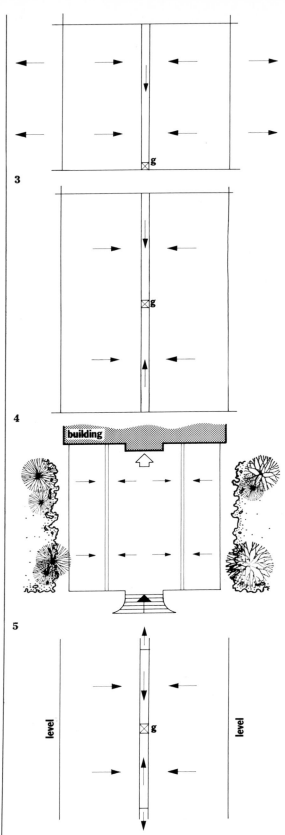

3 *Open channel running to gulley at edge of paving.*
4 *Open channel running to gulley (and soakaway) in paving.*
5 *Open channel, avoiding main traffic route, but parallel to it.*
6 *Where the perimeter is level, falls must be provided in the channels.*

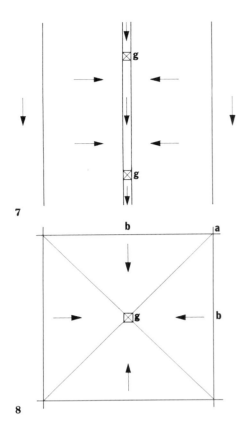

7 *Channel depth can be constant when falls are parallel to the perimeter.*

8 *Cross falls to gulleys. Minimum fall is on line ag and not bg.*

2 Foundations and bedding

2.01 The requirements and methods of bedding for precast concrete units were fully described in *Hard landscape in concrete*. Since substantially similar methods are used for brick paving, the following information is restricted to a summary of the factors involved and to calling attention to aspects or requirements particularly relevant to brick paving.

Choice of base material
2.02 This is primarily a choice between a consolidated hardcore base or a concrete slab, either plain or reinforced. Although there are old brick paved roads which continue to give good service in spite of having only a consolidated earth or hardcore base, any area taking appreciable vehicular traffic should now be laid on a concrete base. For other conditions the choice is more difficult. The tendency in Britain appears to be to have a concrete base in most urban situations, even when the use is solely for pedestrians. The difference in size between bricks and most concrete paving slabs introduces a factor which could influence the choice of base for pedestrian or light wheel traffic situations. The small size brick unit is much less likely to be broken but is rather more liable to settlement. For brick paving, therefore, the choice is often a matter of balancing the extra cost of a concrete base against the acceptability of some displacement.

Factors to be considered
2.03 Determine whether a 'pedestrian' area is accessible to wheeled traffic, recognising that it is difficult to enforce a weight restriction and that a single heavy vehicle can cause trouble. Note, for example, that a pathway available for emergency use of fire services may be used in a practice exercise and not only when a fire occurs.
2.04 What is the character of the finished surface? Displacement of sophisticated flush jointed, smooth faced paving is very obvious and probably unacceptable, whereas minor movement in a rough textured surface might be scarcely noticed.
2.05 Would settlement result in a dangerous surface? This is most likely to apply to busy urban situations. Also important are building exits where there is a sudden change from indoor smooth surfaces to the external paving.
2.06 Will drainage be effective in preventing unacceptable puddles if some settlement occurs? The type of bedding and jointing and the paving falls will affect this.
2.07 Are trenches for drains or other services likely to result in subsidence? As described in *Hard landscape in concrete* all trenches should be correctly filled. It is commonplace for filling to settle slowly and settlement will usually be more apparent in unconcreted areas.

Choice of bedding material
2.08 Some form of cushioning material is necessary between base and paving to refine the finished grade and compensate for any irregularities in the shape of paving units. The choice is between a layer of sand or bedding in mortar. Either may be used above a concrete base. Over a consolidated hardcore base a thick bed of sand seems more suitable than a mortar bed, although the latter is sometimes used.
2.09 Sand bedding is likely to be slightly cheaper in first cost and, where a concrete base is not used, any subsidence faults can be made good relatively easily. Sand bedding allows the paving freedom to move laterally. This obviates the need for special movement joints, except that these are still advisable between large areas of paving and fixed abutments. The freedom to move accentuates the tendency for paving to 'spread' and therefore makes sand bedding a doubtful method except for purely pedestrian use. Edge treatment must ensure that sand bedding will not be washed out.
2.10 When used directly over a consolidated hardcore base sand bedding should probably be about 50 mm thick, as there are likely to be appreciable deviations in the base levels. Over a well-laid concrete slab the sand thickness can be less, with a minimum of 25 mm.
2.11 Mortar bedding is most generally used when laying over a concrete base. The mortar bed is usually 25 mm thick; a cement/lime/sand mix of $1:\frac{1}{4}:3$ is suitable.
2.12 A possible intermediate method, sometimes used over hardcore, is a bedding of lime/sand of $1:4$.

3 Joint material
3.01 The choice is between:
1 tight jointed units without jointing material;
2 joints filled with sand or small shingle;
3 mortared joints.
Choice between these would normally be influenced by:
● appearance, including maintenance;
● whether or not permeability is required for drainage;
● situation and type of traffic;
● cost, including maintenance.
In present day conditions, perhaps the risk of vandalism should be added, as in some locations the easy removal of unmortared paving could provide a ready source of missiles.
3.02 Tight-fitting unjointed paving is feasible only with units of very regular shape and size and is rarely used. Sand or shingle jointing, usually with the joints recessed, can look effective but is probably suitable only for purely pedestrian use and mainly for situations such as parks and gardens in conjunction with the more irregular shaped types of brick. If sand or shingle joints are used enough dirt usually enters the joints to encourage weed growth; periodical weed killer treatment may be needed.
3.03 Mortar joints are normally 10 mm wide, although for some irregular shaped bricks a wider joint may be appropriate.

Narrower joints are possible with regular shaped units but may be difficult to form if the joints are filled by grouting.

Mortared joints

3.04 When constructing brick walls, surplus mortar can cause considerable disfigurement as it is being cut off with a trowel, or when it smears the surface in falling to the ground. With paving, however, the problem is much more acute as all surplus mortar will fall on the finished surface, **9, 10**.

3.05 There are two systems of laying: one the 'bricklayer' method, and the other the 'tiler' method. In the bricklaying method, bedding and jointing is done at the same time. In the tiling method, the units are bedded first and the jointing is done as a separate operation, either by grouting or by brushing into the joints a dry mix and following with a fine water spray. In the latter method further spraying may be needed for two or three days to effect proper curing of the joints. Either method is likely to leave some cement smears on the surface, even with careful workmanship, and if the final appearance is to be satisfactory all the smears must be cleaned off immediately. (An example was seen recently, where an expensive engineering brick edging had been laid around a car parking area. The whole of the brickwork was disfigured by mortar smears which had been allowed to set hard. Two men on their knees were, most ineffectually, scrubbing away. They looked like being there for weeks.)

3.06 Opinions about the respective merits of the two methods vary. It has been argued that with the bricklaying method the immediate formation of the joints ensures better levelling of the units, and, in particular, the avoidance of upstanding arrises when units are somewhat uneven in shape. This would apply mainly with flush jointed work. What is certain is that for a good result high quality workmanship is essential and this seems to be a considerable argument in favour of the use of specialist labour. Ordinary bricklayers are seldom experienced in paving and, even if conscientious, are less likely to do a first class job. The introduction of a 'supply and fix' service by manufacturers, referred to in Chapter 1 para 6.03, page 8, seems a logical approach. The possible use of pre-jointed slabs is an interesting extension of the use of specials which should appreciably reduce the on site jointing difficulties.

3.07 In the United States, elimination of surface disfigurement by mortar is occasionally achieved by coating the top surface of the units with paraffin wax prior to laying. Care has to be taken to avoid the wax getting onto the sides of the units. The wax is subsequently cleaned off by steam.

3.08 For normal techniques, jointing mortar should be 1:3 cement/sand for dry brushed joints or 1:$\frac{1}{4}$:3 cement/lime/sand for grouted joints or joints made by the 'bricklayer' method. Where joints are required to be fully filled, either for appearance or to protect the arrises of the bricks, the choice between a completely flush or a slightly concave finish is a matter of judgment. Either section can be used with regular shaped units but the dished joint may be thought more appropriate for less evenly shaped bricks.

3.09 With any method of mortar bedded or jointed paving the work should be allowed to mature for at least three days before use, even by pedestrians.

Special mortars

3.10 Pre-jointed slab units may take advantage of the development of high bond mortars. Elsewhere there seems little point in using high bond mortar.

3.11 Coloured mortars may be used. For continuity of colour it is safest to use a pre-mix mortar or to rely on colour obtained from the aggregate. Before choosing the colour of jointing, the possible effect of dirt should be considered. Unless paving is regularly cleaned, mortar colour will have less effect on the appearance than it does on vertical work.

4 Recommendations and details

Recommendations

4.01 Recommended bedding and jointing for various applications are shown in table I.

Table I Recommended bedding and jointing for brick pavers

Use	Type of bedding and jointing
1 For most vehicular traffic and busy urban situations	Mortar bedding and jointing of units laid on a concrete base
2 For country car standing areas and for casual or light pedestrian use	Either sand bedding and jointing on a concrete base, or sand bedding and jointing on consolidated hardcore
3 Where direct drainage through the paving is feasible, and use is as in 2	Sand bedding and jointing on consolidated hardcore

9, 10 *Smooth engineering bricks (Preston) are less tolerant of cement smearing than textured, uneven bricks (Marquess Road).*

9

10

1 Functional requirements

Subsidence

1.01 Subsidence is most likely to occur where paving is laid on hardcore without a concrete slab. The cause may be:
● water penetration through the hardcore;
● run-off water breaking down the edge by washing out sand bedding or disturbing the hardcore; or
● excessive loading from unauthorised vehicles (most likely on sharp bends and corners, and in tight parking situations).

Lateral movement

1.02 Where paving width exceeds 10 m, and bedding and jointing is executed in mortar, thermal movement joints should be provided.

1.03 Where paving is sand bedded (whether on a hardcore or concrete base), it tends to spread laterally and, except for very minor paths or small areas, should be provided with restraint at the perimeter.

Levels

1.04 An upstand kerb may be essential as a drainage abutment or for the safety of pedestrians, and may also be a useful deterrent against damage to adjacent grass.

2 Sand bedding on hardcore

2.01 *Planting is approximately level with the edge of paving,* **1**. Surface water drains through the base, and concentrated edge run-off is avoided. Sand bedding is contained by the mortar-jointed brick on end which, in turn, contains the hardcore. The edge bricks are supported by the concrete haunchings, and the foundation provides some safeguard against subsidence. This detail will be satisfactory in most circumstances, but the edge could be damaged by a single heavy vehicle.

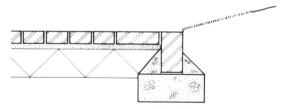

1 *Planting level with paving edge.*

2.02 *Projecting upstand brick kerb, with paving below adjacent ground level,* **2**. Generally comparable with **1**, but the upstand brick on end is less secure, and liable to damage. If the general paving is standard brick on edge, then the kerb height is limited to about 100 mm.

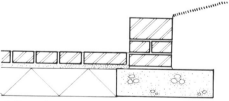

2 *Projecting upstand kerb.*

2.03 *Alternative to* **2**, *with greater support*, **3**. In **1** and **2**, the concrete haunching would not be placed with the foundation. Surfaces are unlikely to be clean, and bond may be poor. By siting the kerb at the edge of the concrete, the haunching may be more substantial than in **2**. Where greater support is considered necessary the addition of dowel pins and rods would help. Dowels should be 12 mm diameter, rods 150 mm long, located at about 600 mm intervals.

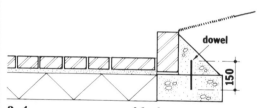

3 *A more secure upstand kerb.*

2.04 *Where an even higher kerb is required,* **4**, a 225 mm dwarf wall may be used without the concrete haunching of **2**.

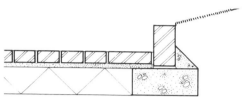

4 *Dwarf wall kerb.*

2.05 Sand bedding and jointing normally make the provision of a thermal movement joint between paving and edging unnecessary. Kerbs and low walls are often laid without movement joints but a simple open joint, through brickwork and the concrete base, at about 10-15 m intervals would be a sensible precaution.

3 Mortar bedded and jointed paving on concrete and hardcore

3.01 *No upstand edge, projection of concrete beyond paved area,* **5**. This common detail protects the edge of the paving from subsidence and from run-off water damaging the foundations, but it inhibits cultivation of the adjacent ground. **6** is probably a better and cheaper alternative.

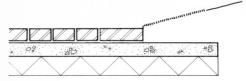

5 *Projecting concrete base.*

3.02 *The thickened concrete edge provides strength*, **6**. It also prevents lateral spread of the hardcore and the ready permeation of run-off water into the paving base. Cultivation of ground adjacent to the paving is not affected.

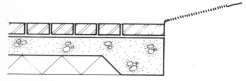

6 *Thickened base at edge.*

3.03 *Upstand edge with no edge drain*, **7**. Concrete haunching might be given dowel support (see **3**). Where paving exceeds 10 m, a movement joint is advised between the paving and the kerb. This joint is shown a brick length away from the kerb rather than immediately adjacent to it. This allows the last paving brick to support the kerb.
Movement joints through the kerb should coincide with joints in the concrete base.

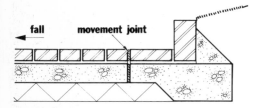

7 *Fall away from edge, across paving.*

3.04 *For where ground fall is parallel to the gutter: upstand kerb and brick dished gutter*, **8**. Unless the general paving is set on very thick bedding it may be necessary to step the concrete below the gutter. The thickened concrete edge of **6** and **7** could equally well be adopted here. Movement joints should not be located parallel with and adjacent to a gutter as the jointing material might become extruded and prevent water run-off into the gutter. This detail is particularly suitable where the paving not only falls towards the gutter, but parallel with it as well.

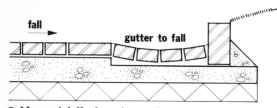

8 *Natural fall of paving and gutter.*

3.05 *Flat gutter for where paving is level parallel to the gutter*, **9**. This is an alternative to **8** for where paving fall is towards the gutter only and fall accommodated in the gutter itself.

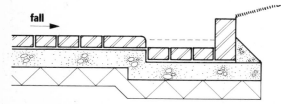

9 *Fall accommodated in gutter.*

4 Appearance requirements

Grass verge levels
4.01 Where paving adjoins grass, the paving or the kerb (if there is one) should always finish below the level of the grass. The difference in level should be determined by the anticipated method of cutting the grass edge, **10, 11,** and **12**. Allowance should be made for the compaction of newly laid soil and grass.

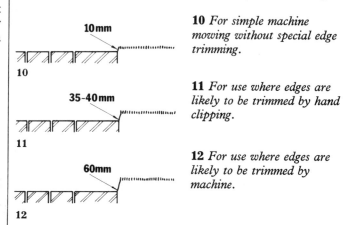

10 *For simple machine mowing without special edge trimming.*

11 *For use where edges are likely to be trimmed by hand clipping.*

12 *For use where edges are likely to be trimmed by machine.*

Restraint for pedestrians
4.02 Requirements at the edge of paved pedestrian areas may vary from those situations where a safety barrier is necessary, to those where unimpeded wandering from paving to grass is acceptable. Often, however, it is desirable to reduce the risk of damage to the grass edge, without forming a real obstruction. A very simple upstand kerb, **13**, has some effect in reducing casual encroachment. It also prevents damage to the upstanding earth edge and is an effective barrier to damage from prams or children's cycles.

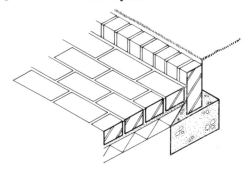

13 *Upstand kerb.*

4.03 Posts of any description, sited either on the grassed area or immediately at the edge of the paving, make machine cutting of the grass impossible. Paving should continue at least 225 mm beyond the line of any obstructions, **14**.

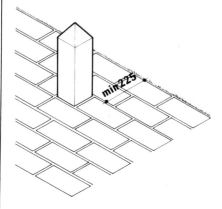

14 *Posts should not impede mowing machine movement along the grass edge.*

4.04 The greatest damage to grass arises from 'corner cutting'. Corners that are generously splayed or radiused help, but in many situations a physical barrier should be considered. A traditional form of deterrent is the 'corrugated' paved surface, separating general paved areas and 'soft' surround. Cobblestones have been one form of this. **15** shows a possible treatment in brick.

Restraint for cars

4.05 The increasing use of brick for car parking surfaces justifies calling attention to a nuisance that is often overlooked. Cars frequently reverse into their parking position and, as a result, cause three types of damage:

● exhaust fumes blacken the structure, causing unpleasant disfigurement;

● careless reversing to the edge of the paved area may cause physical damage to the planting; and

● exhaust fumes may kill all but the most resilient plants.

4.06 A physical obstruction, such as a step which limits car movement, is the only sure preventative. For most cars, an obstruction about 1250 mm from the edge of the paving will suffice **16**.

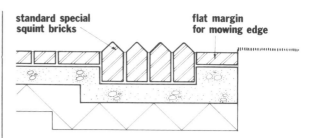

standard special squint bricks   flat margin for mowing edge

15 *Brick 'cobblestones' deter pedestrians from straying on to the grass.*

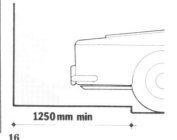

1250 mm min

16

16 *A low kerb will restrict cars, and can control disfigurement by exhaust fumes.*

17 *Where there is little wheeled traffic, and driver behaviour is reliable, the simplest solution is sometimes the most effective: Christ's Hospital, Horsham.*

17

A sloping plinth becomes a major visual feature at Target House, Aylesbury.

Chapter 9: Paving: breaks in the surface; costs

1 Steps

Building regulations

1.01 Steps that do not form part of a building are not controlled by the building regulations.

1.02 External steps that are considered part of a building are those that are necessary to bridge the difference in level between a building and the surrounding ground and/or which take support from the building. These are covered by part H ('Stairways and balustrades') of *The Building (third amendment) Regulations*, 1975. Similar controls apply in Scotland and Northern Ireland. If there is any doubt about interpretation, the local building inspector should be consulted.

1.03 The principal points that will apply in controlled situations are:

● *Pitch.* Stairs (except those serving one dwelling) shall have a pitch not exceeding 38°.

● *2R + G.** The limiting values for this formula are 550 to 700 mm. (This does not allow for very wide treads.)

● *Treads shall be level.* In uncontrolled situations, it may be preferable to have a slight fall, to prevent the retention of water, and possible consequent icing.

● *Width shall be not less than going.* This might inhibit the use of bullnosed bricks, depending on local interpretation.

Design guidance

1.04 In the absence of proper design controls, the building regulations provide a good guide for the design of steps in general landscape work, and the latest requirements, as set

* The 2R + G rule of thumb appears in the table to Regulation H3, under Head G; and definitions of 'going', 'tread' and 'width' in H1. In this chapter 2R + G is expressed as 2R + T where going equals tread (ie where there is no nosing).

out in the third amendment, should be considered in conjunction with the following notes.

1.05 There is usually less need to conserve space outdoors than in internal stairways, and a greater width (front-to-back dimension) of tread will often be more suitable in scale. The 2R + G formula may therefore be used as a guide for many situations, and for determining maximum pitch, but can be dispensed with where the designer wants a free hand to use a low pitch with generous going in casual situations.

1.06 Easy visual identification of the step edge is essential when steps in busy areas are used regularly at night, **1**. Shadows cast by a slight projection will delineate the edge of the tread when ascending, and bond pattern can emphasise the step edge when descending. This latter point is particularly worth exploiting at the top of a flight of steps, **2**.

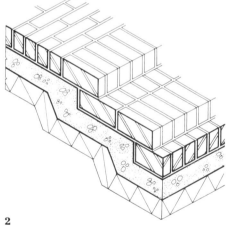

2

1 *Law courts, High Wycombe. The shallow steps are clearly defined, whereas the edge of the shallow ramp to the left might not be seen.*
2 *Top steps accentuated by bond pattern.*

1.07 For simple and economic construction, designers should avoid cut bricks and complicated shaping of the concrete base wherever possible, **3, 4**.

Tread = brick + joint
225 = 215 + 10

Rise = 2 bricks + 2 joints
150 = (2 x 65) + (2 x 10)

2R + T = 525

3

Tread : 215 + 10 = 225
Rise : 102·5 + 65 + (2 x 10) = 187·5

2R + T = 600

4

3 *The concrete is complicated by the two verticals for the steps. This is a rather narrow tread for external use. 2R + T is too small.*

4 *This meets the 2R + T limits but looks mean and is uncomfortably steep for external work. The concrete is complicated, as in 3.*

1.08 Treads should be laid to a slight forward fall. About 5 mm per tread is reasonable in most cases, but this should be increased for very wide treads. Note that these falls will considerably affect the total rise of long flights.

1.09 Rounded nosings are useful in reducing damage (eg outside a hotel luggage doorway), but make identification of the step edge less easy and are not recommended for purely pedestrian situations. If used, the radius of the nosing should be kept small, the BS 'standard special' with a radius of 25 mm being preferable to the 53 mm alternative, **5**.

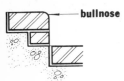
bullnose

5 *These steps have the same dimensions as in 4, but the bullnose reduces the depth of usable tread and the overall going might not be accepted as effective in accordance with the building regulations.*

1.10 Tread units should be laid at right angles to the edge of the step. Thin paver units on risers should always be mastered (ie overlapped) by the tread unit, **6**.

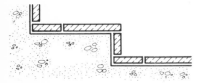

6 *The tread unit must master the riser. Paver dimensions do not necessarily follow BS sizes, therefore dimensions are not shown.*

1.11 Figures **6** to **12** take account of the above factors and show some possibilities. In all except **6**, bricks are assumed to be to BS dimensions and joints are taken as 10 mm. (For simplicity, tread falls are not shown. They would be formed in the bedding process. To obtain the total rise of a flight of steps the 'falls' would need to be added to the 'rise' dimension values shown in the diagrams.)

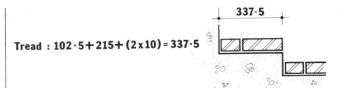

Tread : 102·5 + 215 + (2 x 10) = 337·5

7 *Rise is adjustable. A very generous tread. The exposed concrete needs to be well* *finished, but the change in material helps to define the riser when ascending.*

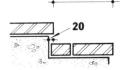

Tread : 102·5 + 215 + (2 x 10) = 337·5
Going : 337·5 − 20 = 317·5

8 *Alternative to 7. By projecting the tread a shadow line is obtained. This adds to the demarcation of the* *riser but does not obviate the need for a good finish to the concrete. The going is 20 mm less than in 7.*

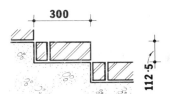

Tread : 65 + 215 + (2 x 10) = 300
Rise : 102·5 + 10 = 112·5
2R + T = 525

9 *A reasonable tread. Although 2R + T is small it would be acceptable, at least for casual situations.* *Risers are not very well defined, and costs would be higher than in an 'on flat' arrangement.*

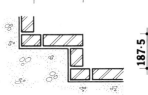

Tread : 37·5 + 10 + 215 = 262·5
Rise : 65 + 102·5 + (2 x 10) = 187·5

2R + T = 637·5

10 *2R + T is rather too big for comfort. Secure fixing of* *riser brick is essential for sound bedding of tread.*

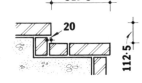

Tread : 102·5 + 215 + (2 x 10) = 337·5
Going : 337·5 − 20 = 317·5
Rise : 37·5 + 65 + 10 = 112·5

2R + G = 542·5

11 *Riser well marked. 2R + G is rather low but* *acceptable for casual leisure areas.*

Tread : 112·5 + 10 + 215 = 337·5
Going : 337·5 − 20 = 317·5
Rise : (2 x 65) + (2 x 10) = 150

2R + G = 617·5

12 *Riser well marked. 2R + G on the high side,* *but deep going makes it acceptable in leisure areas.*

2 Manholes

2.01 Attention was drawn in Chapter 4, page 29, to the importance of the location of manhole covers and of aligning them with paving.

Points of detail to be considered also include:

● The improved appearance obtained if a recessed cover is used, filled with paving units, **13**. Some light inspection covers of the recessed type allow a depth of 30 mm or less for the infill material, which is insufficient even for pavers. Even medium heavy duty recessed covers are unlikely to be deep enough to take standard bricks. An early decision should ensure that either thin pavers or cut bricks can be supplied to match the general paving and that recessed covers are of a suitable depth for units plus bedding material. Where there is not enough depth for a sand/cement bed, pavers can be fixed by the 'thin bed' method, using a suitable adhesive which takes up scarcely any depth.

13 *Recessed manholes at Richard Sheppard Robson & Partners' offices in north London. Note the different colour of the far manhole, possibly caused by the cover retaining moisture after rain.*

(The streamers were temporary!)

● On the outer side of the access cover the frame should either be deep enough for the paving unit and bedding on top of the manhole walling to finish level with the manhole, or the frame should be raised on bedding to provide the necessary depth. Careful supervision is needed to ensure that manhole cover frames are really level with paving. Paving units should be laid with a joint following the line of the outside of the wall of the manhole since, even with good back filling, some differential vertical movement between manhole and surroundings is liable to occur, **14**.

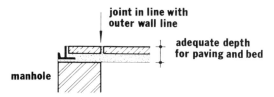

14 *Detailing around manholes should anticipate some differential movement.*

● Where paving is mortar bedded or jointed over a concrete base a movement joint should be formed round the manhole (except with very small areas of paving), **15**.

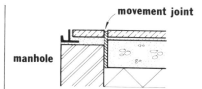

15 *Movement joints should be formed around manholes.*

3 Specification for paving

3.01 Brickwork is not the cheapest form of paving. A decision to use it is generally made because of its attractive appearance. It is therefore important that its visual merits are not spoilt by poor workmanship. Bricks may also be used, in conjunction with special jointing compounds, for their hardwearing and acid resisting qualities. Specifying the type and quality of material is a straightforward matter and a properly complete set of drawings should clarify all construction details. What is more difficult is to convey in the tender documents a description of the standard of finish that is expected, in a way that is both fair to the contractor and that will enable site supervisors to insist on the desired result.

3.02 Reference was made in Chapter 1 (page 5) to the fact that as landscaping is usually carried out towards the end of a contract, there is likely to be considerable pressure to complete quickly. The size and character of the work will influence decisions, but it is suggested that the following aspects should have been considered before the tender stage for brick paving:

1 whether the size, timing, or required quality of work makes the use of a specialist subcontractor advisable;

2 whether quantity and type of paving make it worth investigating the use of precast paver units;

3 the most suitable means for describing quality of workmanship (if completed work of similar character and acceptable quality exists within reasonable distance it may be better to refer to that work than to write a wordy description liable to varied interpretation);

4 whether the 'tiler' or 'bricklayer' method for mortar bedded or jointed paving (see Chapter 7, page 50, para 3.05) is to be laid down by the designer; or whether tendering firms use the method they prefer.

4 Supervision of paving work

4.01 The following matters might be noted as being particularly relevant to paving work:

● Levels should be checked and confirmed before paving work is started. What appear to be reasonable assumptions at early design stage are quite often found to need adjustment. Small changes in levels adjacent to building can seriously affect dpcs and doorways. Ensure that the bottom riser of a flight of steps does not present a hazard because its height differs from other risers.

● Agree on site whether mortar bedded units may, or should, be wetted before laying; it is not necessary or desirable to wet highly vitrified units. Some very absorbent types may need wetting in summer to prevent the mortar drying out too rapidly, resulting in poor bond adhesions. Some manufacturers may advise against wetting because (for their material) it increases the risk of joint discoloration by 'iron staining'.

● For mortar jointed work the responsible site supervisor should be left in no doubt about the need to clean off all mortar droppings or smears before they have set. It is always difficult, and sometimes impossible, to clean properly at a later date.

● Mortar bedded paving should be kept free from all traffic until well set. A three-day traffic free period should generally be insisted upon.

5 Maintenance and cleaning

5.01 Minimal maintenance will be necessary if brick paving is well designed and laid.

Problems encountered
5.02 In reply to questionnaires sent to manufacturers and a limited number of architects the following points were mentioned.

Loosening of mortar joints
5.03 This was mentioned by only one architect. It might be caused by: 1 poor bond resulting from excess wetting of bricks; 2 the opposite extreme of high suction from very dry absorbent bricks; 3 if occurring some considerable time after laying, it could be caused by thermal movement—minor local repair may be needed but serious damage is unusual

Some flaking of bricks
5.04 This was mentioned by a few architects, and is almost certainly due to the use of unsuitable bricks (see Chapter 5, page 42).

Efflorescence or sulphate attack
5.05 There were very few complaints of this. Some temporary efflorescence does occasionally occur, but with bricks of paving quality persistent efflorescence is rare. Bricks of the recommended quality would not suffer sulphate attack but on sulphate bearing subsoils mortar joints or a concrete base could be affected. BRS Digest 90 provides a useful guide on this.

Effect of sea water
5.06 One manufacturer advised against the use of calcium silicate bricks near the sea. Another brick maker made a rather similar comment.

Lichens and mosses causing slipperiness
5.07 This can be a problem in sunless situations in rural areas. It can also occur where a very weak mortar mix has been used (eg 1:3:6). Growth can be killed with a solution of zinc or magnesium silico-fluoride or by proprietary moss killers.
One manufacturer reported best results from spraying with a solution of Thymol-Cresol.

Oil staining
5.08 Sponge or poultice with white spirit, carbon tetrachloride or trichlorethylene.

Tar staining
5.09 Remove as much as possible by careful scraping and then scrub with water and an emulsifying agent. If necessary finally sponge or poultice with paraffin.

Mortar splashes
5.10 Where possible remove large pieces with a scraper and then wash with a dilute solution of hydrochloric acid (1:10 by volume). It is essential to hose well down after an appropriate period (ie when the splashes have dissolved).

Notes on cleaning
5.11 Where any chemical treatment is to be applied the paving should first be saturated with clean water and then after the treatment the brickwork should be thoroughly washed with clean water. Where there is no loose sand, or other loose material, a pressure jet will be the most effective.
5.12 Chemicals will damage grass and plants. Precautions must be taken to restrict chemical spray and to keep run-off, including the cleaning-off water, from reaching grass or plants. If tree roots extend beneath porous paving expert advice may be necessary if serious damage is to be avoided.
5.13 It is generally advisable to treat a small trial area to establish method and suitability.
5.14 Advice on removal of other types of staining, which are less likely to occur on paving than on walls, is given in Practical Note 4 *Cleaning of brickwork* obtainable from the Brick Development Association.

6 Cost factors

6.01 The selection of a type of brick for paving may be controlled more by appearance and performance than individual cost factors, but the costs estimated in table I indicate that the more important considerations are: type of brick used; face size of the unit; transport cost, if the brickworks is some distance away; and method of bedding and jointing (only critical if coloured mortars or complicated patterns are adopted).
6.02 The measured rates given in the table are estimated for 500 m² of straightforward paving, excluding hardcore and/or a concrete base. The supply distance is assumed as being 100 miles, to a provincial town site. Labour rates are taken as 'all-in' rates of £1·82 and £1·45 per hour for craftsman and labourer respectively. No allowances have been made for 'preliminary' items or for profit for the general contractor where work is carried out on a subcontract basis.

Table I Estimated costs of selected types of paving (as at August 1975)

Material type	Material price (£)		Measured rates in £/m²			
	Per 1000		Laid flat		Laid on edge	
	Ex works	Delivered	Mortar bedded and jointed	Sand bedded and jointed	Mortar bedded and jointed	Sand bedded and jointed
Secondhand stocks	57·00	64·77	6·00	5·85	8·60	8·35
Engineering class B	35·00	47·19	5·25	5·05	7·30	7·05
Red pavers 215 × 65 × 33 mm	39·79	44·23	7·20			
Brown pavers 215 × 65 × 33 mm	42·49	46·93	7·40			
Red pavers 215 × 140 × 33 mm	73·17	82·05	5·70			
Brown pavers 215 × 140 × 33 mm	76·00	84·88	5·80			

Chapter 10: Freestanding walls

1 Introduction

1.01 The design of freestanding and earth retaining walls is covered by several British Standards and BS Codes of Practice, and is also the subject of Brick Development Association Technical Note volume 1, number 5. Many of the recommendations made in this and the two following chapters are based on these sources.

2 Special design factors

2.01 Special considerations in the design of external freestanding walls include:

● *rain exposure:* rain may penetrate the wall from both sides and above, affecting both durability and appearance unless brick quality and design detailing take account of the special requirements;

● *thermal exposure:* dpcs in freestanding walls are subject to extremes of temperature, and therefore to high thermal movement;

● *wind exposure:* in a building, a wall of similar height would usually be restrained both at the top and bottom by floors and roof and laterally by cross walls. The freestanding wall, in contrast, is an unrestrained vertical cantilever, and is often designed without any structural calculations having been made;

● *appearance:* there will be two exposed sides to fair-face, unless an applied finish is specified;

● *foundation design:* because freestanding walls do not carry applied loads, there is a tendency to economise on foundation design. This often leads to expensive remedial work;

● *bricklaying in cold weather:* precautions are essential when walls are exposed to wind, rain and frost on both faces;

● *damp proof courses and movement joints:* detailing may differ from the norm in walls of buildings; and

● *associated planting:* adjacent planting may affect detailing, **1**.

1 *Raised planting in the wall dividing the car park at the London Tara Hotel.*

3 Choice of bricks

General

3.01 Brick strength is unlikely to be important. The general factors determining brick choice will be:
1 durability,
2 appearance,
3 cost.

Durability

3.02 Recommendations in CP 121 for clay bricks, and BS 187 for calcium silicate bricks, isolate five conditions:
1 below ground,
2 above ground, up to 150 mm above ground level,
3 bricks used as the dpc,
4 general walling,
5 copings.

3.03 There are also references to work below dpc, but more than 150 mm above ground: it has been assumed that this applies to walls of buildings only, and this category has been excluded from the data given in tables I and II.

3.04 CP 121 (clay bricks) also differentiates between work carried out when there is a risk of freezing, and when there is no risk.

3.05 Tables I and II abstract the information relevant to freestanding walls which are not also earth retaining walls.

Table I Calcium silicate bricks. Quality requirements for durability in freestanding walls.

Position	Brick quality*
Below ground	3 or above
Above ground up to 150 mm	3 or above
Brick dpc	not suitable
General walling	3 or above
Coping	4 or above

* Class as defined in BS 187 Part 2.
NB: For calcium silicate bricks, there should be little problem in choice provided the supplier can match class 3 and class 4 qualities, but on site careful supervision may be needed to ensure that the higher class material is used where required for copings.

Table II Clay bricks. Quality requirements for durability in freestanding walls

Position	Brick quality (Class as defined in BS 3921)	
	No risk of freezing during construction	*Freezing may occur during construction*
Below ground	Ordinary	Special
Above ground up to 150 mm	Ordinary (special preferred)	Special
Brick dpc	Dpc quality, ie engineering class A	Dpc quality, ie engineering class A
General walling	Ordinary	Ordinary
Coping	Special	Special

Suitability

3.06 The recommendations in tables I and II refer only to quality requirements for durability, and are for minimum acceptable standards. The suitability of 'ordinary' quality clay bricks can best be established by consulting the manufacturer or by inspecting examples that have been built for at least three years. This is particularly advisable for work on exposed sites, or in very wet or cold localities.

Appearance

3.07 In addition to normal factors controlling the appearance of fair-faced brickwork, the following special considerations apply to freestanding walls:

● *Matching of brick type:* complying with table II could result in several qualities of brick being used. Dpc and 'special' quality bricks may not be available to match the colour or texture of the preferred 'ordinary' quality material. This would be most apparent if copings were in a different brick.

● *Size:* variation in brick size usually contributes to the attraction of brickwork, but makes it difficult to fair-face freestanding unrendered walls of half, or one-brick thickness. Where one elevation is more important visually, it can be fair-faced at the expense of greater variations in the other face. The BS for clay bricks allows greater variation between individual units than that for calcium silicate bricks. The importance of size variation depends upon the character of the work, but the point should not be overlooked when choosing the materials.

● *Efflorescence:* as a result of high exposure, freestanding walls are more liable to persistent efflorescence than walls in buildings. The BS 3921 requirement for clay bricks of either 'ordinary' or 'special' quality is that the efflorescence should not be more than 'moderate' when tested by the method defined in the BS. Manufacturers should be able to advise, with evidence from built examples, whether their material is of a higher quality than the minimum covered by the BS.

● *Sulphate attack:* freestanding walls are most vulnerable to sulphate action below the dpc and in copings. Avoidance depends upon a correct combination of brick quality and types of mortar. While table II calls for 'special' quality clay bricks for all copings, its acceptance of 'ordinary' quality for general walling is dependent upon an effective dpc immediately below copings, and upon the choice of mortar.

4 Choice of mortar

4.01 Table III (table 6, CP 121) is the basis now generally used for selecting mortars. When designing freestanding walls, the following should be considered:

● *Position in wall:* ie foundation and below dpc, brickwork dpc, general walling and copings.

● *Effectiveness of bond:* the tensile strength assumed when designing high walls by calculation is governed by the effectiveness of the bond between bricks and mortar and dpc and mortar. (See also para 5.06.)

● *Strength of mortar:* a moderately strong mortar is needed in exposed conditions, but this results in relatively poor resistance to cracking. This increases the importance of providing movement joints, especially with calcium silicate bricks.

Table III Equivalent mortar mixes

Mortar designation	Type of mortar (proportions by volume)		
	Cement, lime, sand	Masonry cement, sand	Cement, sand with plasticiser
i	1 : 0-¼ : 3		
ii	1 : ½ : 4-4½	1 : 2½-3½	1 : 3-4
iii	1 : 1 : 5-6	1 : 4-5	1 : 5-6
iv	1 : 2 : 8-9	1 : 5½-6½	1 : 7-8
v	1 : 3 : 10-12	1 : 6½-7	1 : 8

Increased strength; decreased ability to accommodate movements (due to settlement, temperature and moisture changes).

Direction of change in properties → Increasing resistance to damage by freezing

← Improvement in bond and consequent resistance to rain penetration

NB: CP 121 should be referred to for detailed notes regarding the properties of the various mixes and for a general discussion of mortars and their uses.

● *Class of mortar:* table IV shows the minimum class of mortar recommended for each part of the wall. There are three choices of mix (except in designation i). Bond strength may be the most important consideration for high or very exposed walls; frost resistance (by the use of plasticised or masonry cement mortars) may be more important for the average wall of medium height. Designers must find the right balance between the sometimes conflicting advantages of resistance to frost and improved bond strength. Mortar mixes for clay brick walling can be stronger than the minimum shown but the classes indicated for calcium silicate bricks should not be altered. It may be inconvenient to change the mix for different parts of a wall in calcium silicate brickwork, but this is recommended practice.

Table IV Recommended mortar for freestanding walls

Type of brick and position in wall	Mortar class (as table III)	Notes
Foundations and work up to dpc— all brick types	iii	Where sulphates are present in the soil sulphate resisting cement should be used.
Clay brick dpc	i	Ditto
General walling— all brick types	iii	With 'ordinary' quality clay bricks a stronger mortar may be advisable, depending upon the soluble salt content of the bricks or evidence of their behaviour in use. If clay bricks are known to have a high soluble salt content the use of sulphate resisting cement is advantageous.
Copings—clay bricks	i	GLC recommendations advise the addition of a waterproofing agent (eg aluminium stearate) to mortar for clay brick copings.
Copings—calcium silicate bricks	ii	

Joint shape

4.02 Flush, weathered or dished joints are basically suitable, **2**. Choice should depend on brick texture and the desired appearance. Freestanding walls are too exposed for recessed joints to be generally acceptable, **3**.

flush   weathered   dished 'buckethandle'   recessed   reversed struck

2

3

2 *Three acceptable joint shapes.*
3 *Recessed joints are too exposed in garden walls for them to be acceptable.*

5 Damp proof courses

5.01 All freestanding walls (with the possible exception of very low walls built in durable bricks) should include a dpc near ground level.

Position of dpc

5.02 Final ground levels are apt to vary from drawing office assumptions. Dpc levels should therefore be related to actual finished ground levels, allowing for possible differences on opposite sides of a wall. Vertical dpcs should link any change in the level of horizontal dpcs, though they may weaken the bond.

5.03 Where planting adjoins a wall, it is preferable to specify the dpc at 225 mm above ground, rather than 150 mm, to accommodate changes in soil level.

Material

5.04 Although some sheet material dpcs are treated to improve mortar adhesion, most are likely to result in some bond weakening, with two results:

● *reduced resistance to overturning* of the wall by wind, and

● *the formation of a slip plane,* allowing horizontal movements in the upper walling to occur more easily.

5.05 Engineering brick or slate damp courses avoid interruption to bond and should be used for all high walls based upon design calculations which assume the brickwork to take any tension. The height to thickness ratio given in table I, page 65, must be reduced to 75 per cent of the table values where a dpc would not develop adequate bond.

5.06 The slip plane created by sheet material dpcs may be acceptable if the upper walling is generously provided with movement joints, but GLC recommendations specifically warn against the use of bituminous felt, pitch polymer or polythene dpcs in walls of staggered design because of the high risk of cracking arising from rotation at the staggers (see Chapter 11, para 5.07, page 67).

5.07 Where people are likely to lean against parapet walls (eg at view points), there should be a strong bond at the dpc.

Width of dpc
5.08 Where a dpc is of any material other than brickwork, care should be taken to ensure that it extends the full width of the wall. In practice, it is not easy to ensure this and also obtain a neat appearance.

Upper level dpc
5.09 These are closely related to copings, and are considered in the following section.

6 Copings

6.01 The appearance of any wall is affected by its top finish, and this is especially important with freestanding walls, as they are usually seen at close range, **4**.

4 *Freestanding projections to support walls at Sussex University.*

Durability
6.02 The coping is most vulnerable to frost damage, and sulphate attack is also a high risk. The appropriate qualities of bricks and mortar have been given in tables I-IV. Coping units of concrete, cast stone, natural stone and slate are covered in BS 3798.

Protection of wall below
6.03 In addition to the need to protect against direct rain penetration, most authorities recommend that copings should discharge top water by means of a projection and drip. There are many long standing examples, however, of brick copings without an overhang that are satisfactory when appropriate quality materials have been used. The following factors should be considered:

● *Prevention of water penetration:* direct penetration of water to the walling below should be prevented either by an impervious coping (eg metal or plastic), **5**, or by including a dpc beneath the finishing material, **6**. Metal or plastic finishes must prevent penetration at any joints unless a dpc is also included. Joints in these materials need to allow for appreciable thermal movement. Masonry type coping should always be on a dpc because, irrespective of the permeability of the unit, water penetration through mortar joints will almost always occur following thermal or moisture movement.

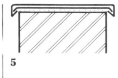
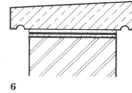

5 *Typical profile for metal or plastic impervious coping.*
6 *Pervious copings must rest on a dpc to ensure protection of wall below.*

● *Run-off water affecting durability:* where general walling uses bricks and mortar of qualities to withstand 'wetting from both sides', it is questionable whether run-off water from copings will significantly affect durability. The worst situation would usually be with impervious cappings of metal or plastic but these are almost invariably designed to project and have relatively good drip shapes. There is also a risk of chemical attack of some bricks by run-off water from limestone and concrete or non-ferrous metals.

● *Run-off water causing disfigurement:* although run-off water may seldom cause deterioration it often results in disfigurement. This is usually seen either as white stains (the result of lime leaching from limestone or concrete copings) or as temporary darkening in colour. The latter can show on any type of brickwork but is likely to be most obvious on even coloured light tone material, especially if the bricks are relatively absorbent. Efflorescence may become a long term nuisance in those bricks vulnerable to it, unless run-off water is directed away from the wall. Projecting copings reduce the risk of disfigurement. Projections, with good drip moulds, should overhang both sides of a wall by at least 45 mm.

● *Falls prevent saturation:* although coping quality should suit exposure conditions, unnecessarily prolonged wetting should be prevented by a fall on the top surface. The fall may be one- or two-way. Where appearance is more important from one direction a one-way slope has a slight advantage, **7, 8**.

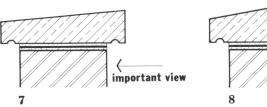

7, 8 *Falls may be one- or two-way.*

● *Bed brick copings to a fall:* although fired clay coping units with shaped tops are included in BS 4729 it appears to be common practice to use standard brick finishes, such as brick-on-edge, bedded level. It would be an improvement to bed them to a slight fall, say 5 mm, **9**.

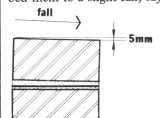

9 *It is preferable to bed brick on edge copings to a slight fall to prevent retention of water and subsequent freezing.*

● *Staining may occur below mortar joints in projecting copings:* streaky marking is liable to occur where water can penetrate through joints in coping projections. With metal or plastic capping systems joints should overlap or be designed to prevent this. Mortar joints in projecting masonry type copings are unlikely to remain waterproof following thermal or moisture movement. The risk of streak staining may be reduced by careful treatment of the dpc.

Position and detail of dpc at copings
6.04 Normally a dpc should be immediately beneath the coping

material and be fully embedded in mortar. Occasionally a dpc is shown one or two courses below the coping. Presumably this is done to try to ensure better bonding of coping to wall but it exposes non-coping material to a very wet situation and is not advisable unless the bricks are of 'special' quality, in the case of clay units, or class 4 if of calcium silicate.

6.05 Dpcs should always extend at least the full width of the walling. Whether they should project is more questionable although most reference sources show them doing so, as in **10**.

10 *Dpcs should project very slightly.*

6.06 The advantage of a projecting dpc shaped as shown would be to divert the water that has penetrated vertical joints of the coping projection. In practice it is difficult, if not impossible, to form the turn-down shape with flexible materials. Also it may be difficult to find ready-cut material of the exact width required. With most types, any attempt to cut on-site is likely to result in a very ragged appearance.

6.07 In a number of continental countries below-coping dpcs are commonly of pre-formed stiff metal—usually zinc. This is evidently considered worthwhile, even on a dwarf wall, **11**. This seems an excellent functional method which, perhaps surprisingly, seems to survive without mischievous or wanton damage. A possible objection to metal dpcs lies in the difficulty in obtaining a good bond between the dpc and the coping. Many continental examples appear to be satisfactory but failures have been seen in the UK, notably where thin coping slabs have been used.

11 *Pre-formed metal coping, seen on the Continent.*

Fixing of copings

6.08 Most masonry type copings are generally secured adequately when properly bedded and jointed in mortar but the following points should be considered:

● *Vandalism:* projections do make it easy to lift all but the very heavy units. Precautions are rarely taken against this risk but it is not difficult to provide a dowel joint between stone or concrete units, giving some extra resistance, **12**.

● *Special risk locations:* where parapet walls may be leant on, or knocked by vehicles, a stepped coping provides a safeguard against accidental dislodgement, **13**.

● *Endfixing:* thermal movement is liable to loosen the end units of brick-on-edge copings. These are usually secured by built-in fish-tailed end cramps of galvanised steel or other non-rusting metal, **14**. The cramps form an ugly feature. A reasonable, but little-used alternative is to form the end of the coping in larger units. Many brick manufacturers could supply units of 215 × 215 mm although, rather surprisingly, they are

not included in BS 4729 *Shapes and dimensions of special bricks* except in the form of double bullnose stop ends.

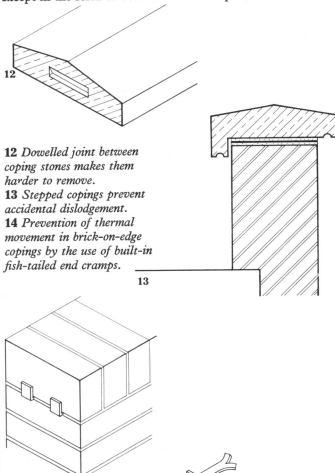

12 *Dowelled joint between coping stones makes them harder to remove.*
13 *Stepped copings prevent accidental dislodgement.*
14 *Prevention of thermal movement in brick-on-edge copings by the use of built-in fish-tailed end cramps.*

Fired clay copings

6.09 BS 4729 includes only two shapes ('half-round' and 'saddleback') and these only to suit 215 mm thick walls. BS 1233 includes further shapes.

6.10 As manufacturers may have other shapes, or may not have readily available a particular shape to match general walling, an early inquiry should be made when fired clay units are likely to be wanted.

6.11 In addition to specially shaped clay coping units it has been common practice to use roofing tiles either as a form of dpc beneath a brick-on-edge finish or more obviously for visual effect. Where tiles are relied on as an alternative to a sheet-type dpc there should be two courses, laid with overlaps to avoid any through joints. Some typical examples are shown in **13-15**.

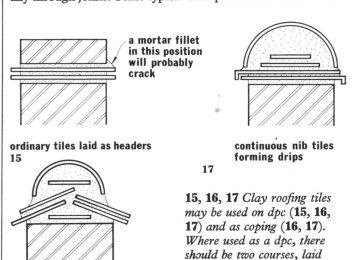

a mortar fillet in this position will probably crack

ordinary tiles laid as headers
15

continuous nib tiles forming drips
17

ordinary tiles laid as stretchers
16

15, 16, 17 *Clay roofing tiles may be used on dpc (15, 16, 17) and as coping (16, 17). Where used as a dpc, there should be two courses, laid to overlap.*

Above: Warwick Road, London. Housing, built on a deck over a vehicle servicing depot, includes landscaped areas; the stepped brickwork up to the planted bed provides casual sitting facilities.

Below: Portsmouth city centre redevelopment. A variant on square topped brick as coping for low walls. Note inclusion of a vertical joint to accommodate movements.

Chapter 11: Stability of freestanding walls

1 Factors affecting stability

1.01 This section deals with the design of normal freestanding brick walls where empirical methods will usually suffice. Detailed calculations would be done by an engineer.

1.02 Although in many cases, the ratio of height to width (slenderness ratio) is the major factor affecting stability, the complete list of criteria could include:

- wall plan shape (**2.01**)
- type of bond (**2.02**)
- use of reinforced brickwork (**2.04**)
- weight of brick type (**2.05**)
- slenderness ratio (**3**)
- wind load (**3**)
- load imposed where the wall acts as a retaining wall due to changes in ground level (**3.03**)
- movement joints (**5**)
- suitable foundations (**6**)
- special strength requirement (**7**).

2 Preliminary design considerations

Plan shape

2.01 While stability against lateral wind load may be obtained solely by employing the slenderness ratio, it may be more economical to incorporate projecting buttresses or provide stiffening, by using staggered, bent or curved shapes, **1**.

The effect of bond pattern

2.02 Any of the normal bond patterns may be used on solid, unreinforced walls. The differences between them have little effect. Where there is only one fair face, the 'garden wall' bond will be more economical in walls more than one brick thick.

2.03 One traditional bond that appears to have gone out of use is 'rat-trap', **2**. This bond saves 25 per cent in material in a wall one brick thick. The reduced weight may impair stability, compared with a solid wall of the same thickness, but from the recommendation in CP 121, it appears that the slenderness ratios (table I) could be used for rat-trap bond. Alternatively, height could be limited to about 80 per cent of the acceptable maximum for a comparable solid wall.

Reinforced brickwork

2.04 With reinforced brickwork, the reinforcement will be used mainly as vertical bars. Reinforced concrete cavity fill construction is an obvious system, **3**. A possible alternative is quetta bond, **4**.

Weight of brick type

2.05 Although weight is an important factor, the differences between brick types are normally ignored when using empirical methods of design.

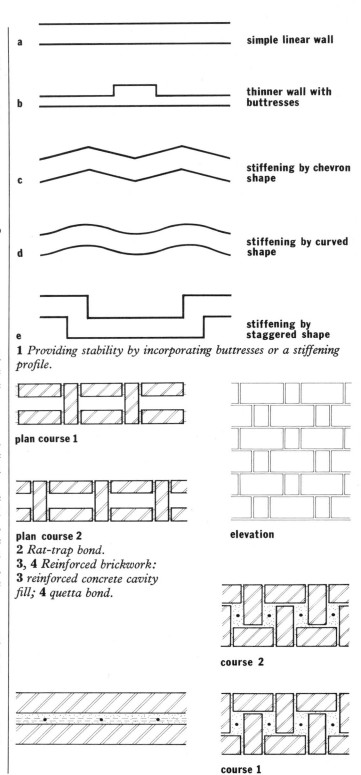

a simple linear wall

b thinner wall with buttresses

c stiffening by chevron shape

d stiffening by curved shape

e stiffening by staggered shape

1 *Providing stability by incorporating buttresses or a stiffening profile.*

plan course 1

plan course 2

elevation

2 *Rat-trap bond.*
3, 4 *Reinforced brickwork:*
3 *reinforced concrete cavity fill;* **4** *quetta bond.*

course 2

course 1

3

4

3 Empirical design method: exposed situations

3.01 High walls, or walls of moderate height in very exposed situations, should be designed by calculation using CP 111 design methods and CP 3: chapter 5 for wind loading data. For most walls, however, it will be more convenient to use the empirical methods and table I gives the necessary information once a design wind speed has been assessed.

Table I Height to thickness ratio related to wind speed			
Design wind speed m/sec	Wind pressure N/m²		Height to thickness ratio
Up to 20	Up to	285	Not exceeding 10
28		575	7
34		860	5
38		1150	4

Factors affecting calculations

3.02 In using table I, there are two things to consider:

● *Effect of the dpc:* if there is a horizontal dpc near the base of the wall which prevents the development of vertical tension, the minimum thickness should be the greater of either

a the appropriate height/thickness ratio × ¾, and the height of the wall above dpc, or

b the appropriate height/thickness ratio calculated with the height of the wall taken from the lowest level at which the wall is restrained laterally by the earth.

● *Effect of wind speed:* wind speed can have a considerable effect on loading calculations, and the designer must make a careful estimate. The method for assessing wind speed is set out in CP 3: chapter 5 but evaluation is not without its problems.

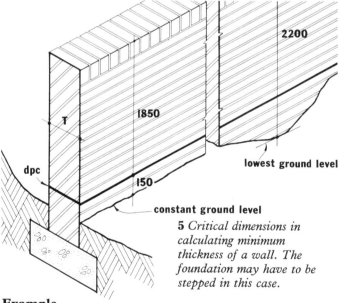

5 *Critical dimensions in calculating minimum thickness of a wall. The foundation may have to be stepped in this case.*

Example

3.03 The minimum thickness of a wall, **5**, would be calculated as follows:

If the design wind speed is known to be 32m/sec, and the height of the wall is to be 2000 mm, we know from table I that the slenderness ratio must not exceed 5. From the ratio we can determine wall thickness. Slenderness ratio = height thickness (SR = H/T)
therefore T = H/SR.
= 2000/5
= 400 mm.

But, if the wall has a dpc near ground level which allows the upper part of the wall to move in isolation, we must choose the greater figure given from **a** or **b** (from para 2.02)—

a SR × ¾ = H (dpc)/T
(this formula requires the height of the wall above dpc level—say, 1850 mm)

5 × ¾ = 1850/T
T = 1850/5 × ¾
= 499·33 mm if there is a dpc near ground level

b SR = H (greatest)/T
(this formula calls for the height above lowest level of restraint—say, 2200 mm)

5 = 2200/T
T = 2200/5
= 440 mm if a wall has no dpc at ground level

(All these figures must be rounded up to rational brick sizes.) The large wall widths produced by this method of calculation result from the high wind exposure conditions. Compare them with the thicknesses acceptable in GLC areas, **6** to **12**.

4 GLC design method: sheltered positions

4.01 Where the site is in a sheltered position, comparable to a well built up area, we could use the design method published by the Brick Development Association and used within the GLC. This method is detailed below.

Basic rules

4.02 The main rules controlling the design of boundary walls are:

a Walls over 1800 mm in height should be referred to a structural engineer for checking.

b Walls which may form part of future garages should be referred to a structural engineer for checking.

c Walls between 900 and 2700 mm in height must be built in accordance with figs **6-12** (boundary walls in excess of 1800 mm are to have the approval of the district surveyor in the GLC area).

d Walls with piers up to and including 900 mm height may be built without short returns (or staggers) in single leaf brickwork not less than 100 mm thickness.

e The dpc at the base of the wall shall be two courses of bricks having an absorption not greater than 4·5 per cent set in 1:3 sulphate-resisting Portland cement/sand mortar; alternatively, two layers of slate may be used as recommended in BS 743: 1951.

f It may be necessary to adjust the suction rate of some clay bricks by wetting or using a water retentive mortar.

g Joints must be pointed as the work proceeds with a flush, weathered or ironed joint.

h Walls constructed of bricks of ordinary quality must be provided with an adequate coping. In areas where the incidence of frost is high, an overhanging coping must be used.

Mortar mixes

4.03 Mortar mixes for clay bricks should be:

a *Clay bricks of ordinary quality* (clay bricks of ordinary quality may not be satisfactory in some situations outside the GLC area and if any doubts exist the brick manufacturer should be consulted):

● from foundation to 150 mm above ground level 1:3 sulphate-resisting Portland cement/sand mortar;

● from 150 mm above ground level to the underside of the coping 1:6 sulphate-resisting Portland cement/sand mortar with approved plasticiser (eg vinsol resin);

● coping 1:3 waterproofed cement (eg addition of aluminium stearate)/sand mortar.

b *Clay bricks with a low soluble sulphate content or clay bricks of special quality:*

● from foundation to 150 mm above ground level 1:3 Portland cement/sand mortar;

● from 150 mm above ground level to the underside of the coping 1:1:6 Portland cement/lime/sand mortar or 1:6 Portland cement/sand plasticised mortar;

● coping 1:3 waterproofed cement/sand mortar.

Testing

4.04 Samples of all mortars should be checked regularly.

Precautions

4.05 Points of special consideration are:

a It is not recommended that staggered walls be used in conjunction with bituminous felt, pitch polymer or polythene dpcs as cracking is likely to occur due to rotation at the 'staggers' or short returns (see CPTB Technical Note Volume 1, Number 10 *Movement joints in brickwork*).

b With this type of construction it is particularly desirable to have movement joints at close centres (ie 6-12 m) carefully positioned, so as not to impair the stability of the wall.

Walls up to 900 mm above ground

215 piers at 1800 centres

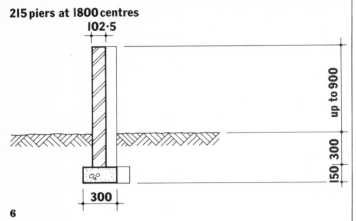

6

Walls between 900 and 2100 mm high

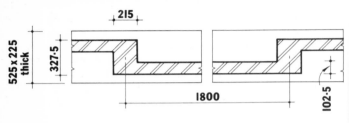

7a

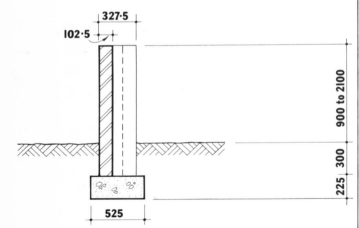

7b

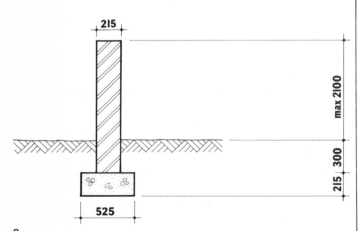

8

Staggered walls: dimensions and bonds

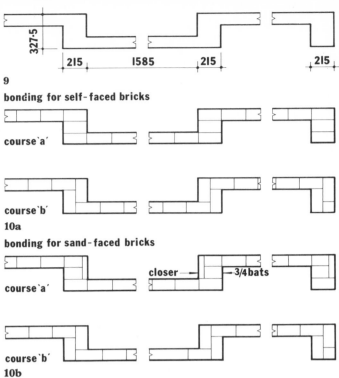

9

bonding for self-faced bricks

course 'a'

course 'b'

10a

bonding for sand-faced bricks

course 'a'

course 'b'

10b

Walls between 2100 and 2700 mm high

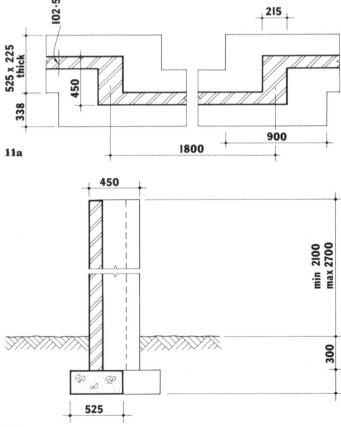

11a

11b

6 *Recommended dimensions for garden walls up to 900 mm above ground.*
7, 8 *Recommended dimensions for walls between 900 and 2100 mm: **7** staggered wall, **8** straight wall. The foundations shown in **7b** and **8** are suitable if the allowable ground pressure is not less than 80 kN/m².*

9 *Setting out dimensions for staggered walls.*
10 *Bonding: **a** self-faced bricks, **b** sand-faced bricks where appearance of sand-faced header on the garden elevation is not acceptable. Alternatively, one sand-faced header can be sanded off on site. The queen closer in **10b** is unacceptable: it could be replaced by two half bats.*
11, 12 *Walls over 2100 mm: **11** staggered wall, **12** (opposite) straight wall.*

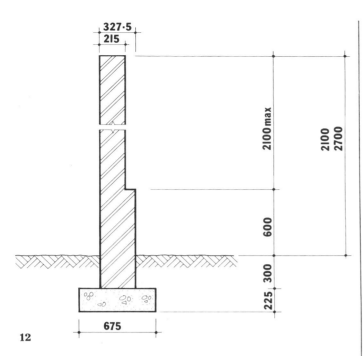

327·5
215

2100 max

2100
2700

600

300
225

675

12

5 Movement joints in freestanding walls

5.01 Although many old walls without movement joints have proved satisfactory, this is almost certainly because they were built in weak lime mortar. A stronger mortar, used as recommended in paragraph **3.03**, necessitates movement joints.

5.02 CPTB Technical Note Number 10 (now obtainable from BDA) deals at some length with movement joints in brickwork but the important factors of frequency and location are discussed here.

Frequency

5.03 Vertical joints to accommodate horizontal movement are recommended at about 12 m intervals in clay brick walls and at about 7 or 8 m intervals in walls of calcium silicate or concrete bricks.

Location

5.04 In simple walls the location of movement joints presents no problem but for walls relying upon buttresses or wall plan shaping, a vertical break may critically effect stability.

5.05 If long wall C relies for stability on buttress B, **13**, a vertical break in its length or at its junction with one or both buttresses would render it unsafe. The joint must therefore be through a buttress (ie forming two buttresses instead of one, each adequately sized to support its adjoining wall), **14**.

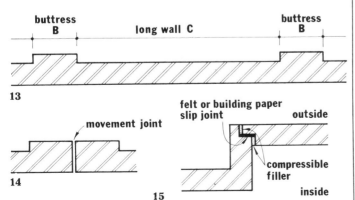

buttress
B

long wall C

buttress
B

13

movement joint

14

felt or building paper
slip joint

outside

compressible
filler

inside

15

13 If a wall achieves stability by being buttressed, 13, movement joints must not negate the structural integrity by separating the wall from its buttresses. Two buttresses (one either side of the joint) must be formed wherever a movement joint is required, 14.
15 This joint is acceptable in short return staggers.

5.06 With a staggered wall, the movement joint becomes more difficult. For short return walls of buildings a joint similar to **15** is suitable as the shape allows external wind pressure to be transferred.

5.07 With a freestanding wall subject to pressure from either side, this form is not acceptable where the main walls rely upon the 'stagger' for stability.

5.08 In the GLC guide the staggered form is shown only for half-brick thick walls and a note says 'with this type of construction it is particularly desirable to have movement joints at close centres (ie 6-12 m) carefully positioned, so as not to impair the stability of the wall'. An answer to the conundrum is not offered in the guide.

5.09 It appears that to include movement joints without losing lateral stability an arrangement using doubled end returns, as **16**, would be necessary. With this complication the value of the 'staggered' form becomes less than at first sight appears.

Type of joint

5.10 Most references illustrate movement joints comprising a compressible filler with mastic seals, either as a straight joint, **17**, or as a staggered joint, as in **15**.

In buildings, where prevention of water penetration is essential, this type of joint is necessary but it seems questionable whether it is needed with freestanding walls. Filling and sealing are costly, and vulnerable to damage. An open joint, larger than would allow ice to form in the cavity (8-10 mm) might be used.

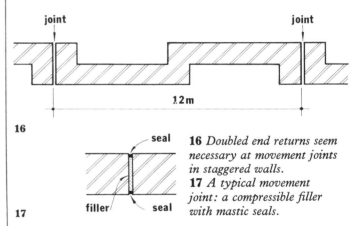

joint

joint

12 m

16

seal

filler

seal

17

16 Doubled end returns seem necessary at movement joints in staggered walls.
17 A typical movement joint: a compressible filler with mastic seals.

6 Foundations

6.01 In theory, all wall foundations should follow the general rules. In practice, there is a considerable temptation to economise in landscape work, especially with regard to total depth of foundation below ground level.

Depth of foundations

6.02 In most cases, the important consideration will be whether the foundation is at a depth which will prevent seasonal movement, rather than its ability to spread loads over a safe bearing area. The depth shown in **6** should be regarded as the minimum, except for very minor dwarf walls. For high walls on heavy clay soils a greater depth should be considered. (750 mm is commonly recommended for walls of buildings founded on clay.)

6.03 For very low walls where economy may be more important than a risk of some movement, excavation might stop at the underside of top soil.

Trees

6.04 The damage that can be caused by rapidly growing trees or by changing soil conditions following removal of large existing trees is relevant. Where this risk can be foreseen, foundations need special consideration, perhaps being increased in depth or strengthened by reinforcement.

7 Ground level parapet walls

7.01 The term 'parapet wall' is used here to mean a low wall sited where there is a substantial difference between ground levels on the two sides of the wall.

7.02 Safety requirements refer to height and stability and restrict opening sizes to prevent accidents to children. The building regulations require a minimum height of 1·1 m for balustrades but this may not always be adequate, especially where children may be without supervision. A small child can be very frustrated by being unable to 'see over'. It is difficult to combine a solid brick wall with a rail above that does not positively entice children to climb dangerously, **18**.

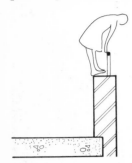

18 Solid parapet walls having a top rail within reach will be climbed.

Accommodating lateral loads

7.03 No brick parapet wall should be less than 200 mm thick. Where there is even a remote chance of a crowd gathering, and leaning against the parapet, special consideration is necessary. Extra stability might be provided by reinforced brickwork designed as cantilever construction. For plain brickwork the design may either be calculated by neglecting tensile value and using only dead weight and thickness to resist overturning (a factor of safety of 2 is normal), or may assume a maximum tensile stress of $0·07$ MN/m^2 where materials and conditions justify (see CP 111) by designing the wall as a cantilever.

8 Perforated walls

8.01 There is little authoritative guidance on the design of perforated screen walls, but it is reasonable to assume that in most cases the reduction in weight would be offset by the reduction in wind load.

9 Wall corners

9.01 Brickwork is often described as having a 'friendly' appearance but an exposed right angle can be anything but friendly in some circumstances. In children's play areas or where hurrying people on fairly narrow walkways have to negotiate a corner the sharp angle could advantageously be eliminated. There are many possibilities, from the simple introduction of bullnose or cant bricks, **19**, **20**, to building the wall with a radiused corner, **21**, **22**.

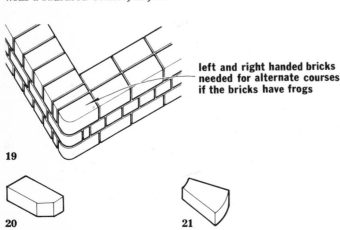

left and right handed bricks needed for alternate courses if the bricks have frogs

19 Wall corners built with bullnose or cant bricks, 20.
21 Radial header brick.

9.02 BS 4729 includes radial header bricks. Manufacturers may be able to supply these in various shapes to provide an outer diameter varying from 1·75 to 5·0 m.

9.03 Where wider than normal vertical joints are acceptable a radiused wall can be built with standard rectangular bricks. If through-the-wall headers are used the diameter the wall follows becomes quite considerable if joints are to be kept within reasonable limits. But if stretchers are used a diameter of 4 m or rather less seems feasible, **22**. In a one brick thick wall this means building the corner as two half-brick walls. The strength resulting from this wall shape is acceptable in most cases of plain brickwork, but wall ties or mesh reinforcement could readily be included if thought necessary.

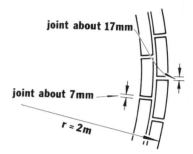

joint about 17mm

joint about 7mm

r = 2m

22 Corner in stretcher bond. The shape may be stiff enough to ensure stability, but ties or mesh reinforcement may be added.

10 Junctions of freestanding walls to buildings

10.01 Where garden walls meet buildings, differential settlement is likely to occur. As rain exclusion at the junction is not essential it is generally more sensible to design the garden wall as a self-supporting structure, separated from the building, including carrying the separation down through the foundation.

11 Gardening aspects

11.01 Planting details tend to be left until a late stage. The following points should at least be considered, and where possible, be discussed with any appointed horticulturalist, in time to incorporate any external works required in the building contract:

● **Frost:** as many gardeners know to their cost, frost pockets are a menace. On sloping sites, frost flows downhill and collects behind any solid obstruction. A brick wall with some low level perforations may be preferred to solid construction.

● **Wind shelter:** a high solid obstruction in an exposed situation does not provide the wind shelter that might be expected, **23**; indeed, a hedge is often better than a solid wall. A perforated wall might be more acceptable.

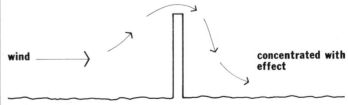

wind

concentrated with effect

23 A high solid wall does not give wind shelter on the leeward side. The wind accelerates over it, and causes considerable turbulence.

● **Effect of planting on foundation depth:** where climbing plants are intended or where any moderately deep rooting plants will be close to a wall foundation depth may need to be increased, while width should be restricted to the minimum essential for stability.

● **Built-in plant fixings:** for climbing plants vine nails or other fixings to take wires are likely to be used. It is better for these to be built-in rather than driven in at a later date.

Above: Andover town centre. Paving, walls and planting form a pleasant resting area, away from the mainstream of the traffic.

Below: Dry brick flower beds. Suitable for temporary or permanent features, and an ideal 'Do-It-Yourself' garden feature.

Chapter 12: Retaining walls

1 Introduction

1.01 The walls considered here are those which act as earth retaining structures for part or the whole of their height on one side while being exposed on their opposite side. Retaining walls forming part of buildings are not considered.

Differences between retaining walls and freestanding walls

1.02 The major differences from freestanding walls are:
● The significant lateral loading is from the earth for the height to which a wall is earth retaining. Wind load on the opposite face becomes unimportant.
● Unless fully protected by waterproofing between wall and earth (unusual for landscape walls), retaining walls will remain damp for longer periods than freestanding walls. The exposed side may therefore be subject to more risk of frost damage, although this risk may be offset by the heat retaining potential of the earth backing.
● Unless fully protected by waterproofing between wall and earth, the wall will be exposed to the transfer of soluble salts during long periods of dampness. This increases risk of sulphate action and of prolonged efflorescence.
● Water draining from retained earth towards a wall may be trapped by the wall and, as a result, penetrate to the foundations, affecting the stability.

2 Special requirements

2.01 Except for references to wind loading, many of the recommendations for freestanding walls are applicable but the above factors impose some additional requirements, **1**:

Brick quality
2.02 Assuming that the backs of walls are not fully waterproofed but that reasonable drainage is provided:
● Calcium silicate bricks should be to BS 187 Class 4 quality or above.
● Clay bricks should be to BS 3921 'special' quality.

Mortar
2.03 For calcium silicate brickwork mortar should be class ii (table III in Chapter 10, page 60).
For clay brickwork mortar should be class i.
If retained earth contains soluble sulphates the cement should be sulphate resisting rather than ordinary Portland.

Back drainage and protection
2.04 Backs of walls are often not waterproofed. A useful compromise, at reasonable cost, is to treat the back of a wall with bituminous paint or line it with heavy polythene sheet.
2.05 Good drainage should be ensured whether or not the back of a wall is waterproofed. Back fill should be permeable material with drainage at least at low level. The fill material may be broken stone or clean broken brick. Old bricks with a high sulphate content or contaminated with gypsum plaster should not be used.
2.06 Drainage may be by small pipes, laid to slope down towards the exposed wall face and projecting slightly beyond it, say 40 mm.
2.07 If drainage is by a land drain laid at the base of the back filling, the drain should not only be laid to falls but must be carried to an effective outlet. As land drains do not always remain effective some drainage outlets through the wall as an additional precaution are advised. Where walls retain a considerable height of earth, some outlets at mid-height, in addition to those just above ground level, may be advantageous.

Damp proof courses
2.08 Although walls may absorb water seeping from the fill, it is still worth preventing unnecessary rain entry through copings. A dpc should be provided as for freestanding walls.
2.09 It seems questionable to provide a dpc near to the exposed side ground level, except where the back of a wall is effectively waterproofed. What is important is that if a low level dpc is used it should be of bricks or slates. Other types are liable to form a slip joint allowing the upper walling to move outward under lateral pressure.

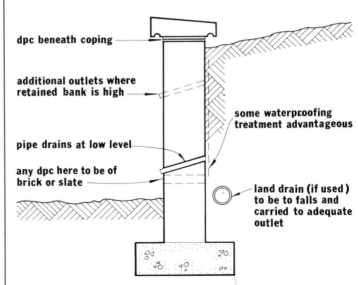

dpc beneath coping

additional outlets where retained bank is high

some waterproofing treatment advantageous

pipe drains at low level

any dpc here to be of brick or slate

land drain (if used) to be to falls and carried to adequate outlet

1 *Main characteristics of a brick retaining wall: coping with dpc; low level dpc to be of brick or slate; drainage through, and at back of, wall; and waterproofing at the back of the wall.*

3 Design of retaining walls

Wall strength

3.01 Unreinforced retaining walls must have sufficient weight and thickness to resist overturning, with a factor of safety of 2. For simple straight walls this leads to the middle third rule,† where no tension is developed at the back of the wall, **2**. Where quality of materials and workmanship ensure good bond between bricks and mortar and no loss of bond due to a dpc, an alternative is to assume a tension of 0·07 MN/m².

Rule of thumb

3.02 A rule of thumb often used for walls up to 2 m high is for the unsupported height not to exceed four times the wall thickness.

GLC design method

3.03 The GLC guidance, as detailed in BDA Technical Note Vol 1 Number 5 July 1972 *The design of freestanding brick walls* is as follows:

Table 1 Design method for retaining walls*

Height of wall above ground	Height of wall from top of foundation	Thickness of wall	Width of foundation		Thickness of foundation
			110 kN/m²	55 kN/m²	
h max mm	H mm	t mm	W mm	W mm	D mm
900	1 125	215	525	525	225
1 200	1 425	327·5	600	600	225
1 500	1 725	440	675	900	225
1 800	2 025	552·5	750	1 050	225

* The above data is based on the following:
● Safe minimum bearing pressures: granular soil 110 kN/m², cohesive soil 55 kN/m².
● No dpc (other than dpc bricks or slates at low level).
● Minimum crushing strength of bricks 20·5 MN/m².
● Mortar mix—1:1/4:3 Portland cement lime sand.

Notes
1 In sulphate bearing ground or when the bricks have a high soluble sulphate content a sulphate-resisting cement should be used for the concrete and mortar; alternatively a richer mix based on ordinary Portland cement.
2 In very wet conditions a French drain should be provided.
3 Brick veneers may be included in the wall thickness (t) if the normal wall tie spacings are halved.
4 Masonry cement and plasticisers should not be used.
5 The wall may be of uniform thickness throughout or be stepped as shown in **3** and **4**.
6 Movement joints are to be provided at centres not exceeding 15 m.

3.04 Rule of thumb methods assume there is no surcharge. (The GLC assumes earth slope upward from the wall does not exceed 1:10.) What is seldom pointed out is that earth levelling may well be carried out by heavy plant operating close to a new wall on the upper earth level side. Without adequate protection from temporary shores against this temporary but high additional surcharge, failure is likely.

Design by calculation

3.05 For all but simple cases such as those covered in table I, retaining walls should be designed by calculation based upon reliable information, such as that contained in the Institution of Civil Engineers *Earth retaining structures*, Civil Engineering Code of Practice Number 2 1951.

3.06 Where a brick face is required, but loading is too great for simple brickwork to be economic, it is possible to use a shaped wall profile to give added strength, reinforced brickwork using special bonds or reinforced concrete cavity fill. It should be noted that if wall ties are used they will be subject to more severe conditions than normal. The GLC suggests using stainless steel or non-ferrous ties. For a good brick face and high lateral loading a reinforced concrete inner wall separated from the brick facework by a cavity may be a sensible composite solution. Properly constructed, this could make the substitution of good 'ordinary quality' clay bricks for 'special' quality acceptable.

† Middle third rule: one-third the width of the section, centrally disposed. Provided the line of resultant pressure lies wholly within it, no tensile forces come into play.

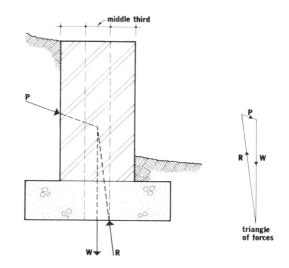

2 *The middle third rule, although more applicable to simple mass concrete retaining walls, can be interpreted by calculating the triangle of forces. Earth pressure P and weight of wall W cause a reaction R under the foot of the wall. R is obtained by plotting P and W to scale and inclination in the triangle of forces. The ends are joined to give the scale and direction of R.*

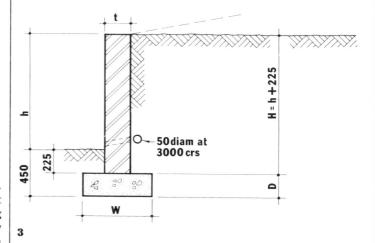

3

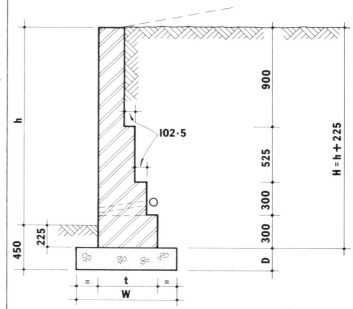

3, 4 *The GLC method of design for freestanding walls may be applied to walls of uniform thickness, **3**, or stepped walls, **4**.*

4 Movement joints

4.01 Thermal movement in earth retaining walls will be less than in freestanding walls but there is a greater risk of moisture movement, and movement joints are still advisable for long walls. The spacing of 7-9 m recommended for freestanding walls in calcium silicate brickwork should not be increased. With clay brickwork spacing might be rather greater than the 12 m suggested for freestanding walls but there does not appear to be any reliable data on this.

4.02 If a wall extends above the highest ground level to become exposed on both sides, movement joints should be as for freestanding walls.

4.03 The effect of movement joints upon strength should be considered, particularly where strength is achieved by shape in the form of return walls. Movement joints also allow considerable water penetration, making effective waterproofing even more difficult. The use of a fully open joint, as discussed in the last chapter, may be unsuitable as earth could wash through. **5** and **6** illustrate two possible solutions.

bituminous felt

open movement joint with bitumen felt restricting earth escape

5

sheet material slip joint

open joint with 'tight' stagger and a slip material

6

5, 6 *Methods of preventing earth washing through open movement joints.*

5 Planting troughs and low walls

5.01 Low walls for planting troughs etc, **7**, are often required to match nearby buildings and a change from 'ordinary' to 'special' quality bricks may be inconvenient. Full waterproofing of the inside of the walls is often a reasonable answer. The treatment should be able to withstand damage during cultivation. A slate lining is probably most effective although a carefully applied waterproofed cement rendering can be reasonably successful.

5.02 Both the wall and the planting will benefit from weepholes, placed at about 2 m centres, unless sub-soil drainage is known to be very good.

7 *A simple retaining wall used to define a change in level.*

Paving outside the Law Courts, High Wycombe.

References

The references given here include only the main sources of information used.

Statutory instruments
HMSO, 49 High Holborn, London, WC1V 6NB
● SI 1972, No 317, Building and buildings. *The Building Regulations* 1972, HMSO (plus Amendments SI 1973 No 1276, SI 1974 No 1944 and SI 1975 No 1370)
● SI 1971, No 2052 (S218), Building and buildings. *The Building Standards (Scotland) (consolidated) Regulations* 1971, HMSO (plus Amendments SI 1973 No 794 (S65), SI 1975 No 404 (S51))

British Standards Institution
101 Pentonville Road, London, N1 9ND
● CP 3: Chapter V: Part 2: 1972, Wind loads. £9·20
● CP 111: Part 2: 1970, Structural recommendations for loadbearing walls, metric units. 75p
● CP 121: Part 1: 1973, Walling, brick and block masonry. £9·20 (plus Amendment AMD 1751, May 1975. £1·50)
● BS 187: Part 2: 1970, Calcium silicate (sandlime and flintlime) bricks, metric units. £2·40 (plus Amendment AMD 695, February 1971)
● BS 3921: 1974, Clay bricks and blocks. £5·80
● BS 4729: 1971, Shapes and dimensions of special bricks. £2·40

Building Research Establishment
Available from HMSO
● Digest 77 (second series), December 1966, Damp proof courses

● Digest 89 (second series) January 1968, Sulphate attack on brickwork
● Digest 160 (second series) December 1973, Mortars for brickwork

Brick Development Association
19 Grafton Street, London, W1X 3LE
● *The brick bulletin* (illustrations from numerous issues have been used)
● Technical Note Volume 1, No 5, July 1972, K. Thomas and J. O. A. Korff *The design of freestanding brick walls*
● Technical Note Volume 1, No 7, May 1973, K. Thomas and L. Bevis *Brick floors and brick paving*
● Practical Note 2, September 1973 *Mortars for brickwork*
● Practical Note 4 *Cleaning of brickwork*
● Brick Information Sheet No 7 *Brick shapes—copings* (originally published by the National Federation of Clay Industries)
● C. C. Handisyde and B. A. Haseltine *Bricks and brickwork*. 1974. £7·50

Other publications
● Elizabeth Beasley *Design and detail of space between buildings*. Architectural Press. 1960 (out of print)
● William Frost and R. V. Boughton *Modern practical brickwork*. Batsford. 1954 (out of print)
● Brick Institute of America *Brick floors and pavements*. Technical Note 1975
● *Handbook of urban landscape* editor Cliff Tandy. Architectural Press. 1972. £7·50
● Maritz Vandenberg and Michael Gage *Hard landscape in concrete*. Architectural Press. 1975. £6·95

Appendix

Notes on the applicability of information to work outside the United Kingdom

A Choice of bricks
Local standards should be consulted for information on commonly available sizes but, as in the United Kingdom, manufacturers may also provide non-standard sized units.

The basic principles on quality requirements discussed in this book should apply in most geographical locations but detailed advice such as that related to particular BS quality will not be of direct use. In the USA the wide variations in climate include not only regions having from mild to very cold winters but also cold areas which differ significantly in their effect on brick durability according to the rainfall and the number of freeze/thaw cycles. American National Standards for facing bricks, such as ASTM 216 for clay bricks and ASTM C 73 for calcium silicate bricks, are of some help although, as in the UK, evidence of behaviour under local conditions over a period of not less than three years is likely to be the most reliable guide. American Standard 37.15 for Paving Bricks includes a wear test but not an exposure test. The Brick Institute of America (1750 Old Meadow Road, McLean, Virginia 22101) issues Technical Notes, and Number 14, Part 1 of *Brick Floors and Pavements* includes some advice on quality while confirming that evidence of in-use performance is at present the best guide.

B Metric conversion factors

Basic units

				Additional familiar units		
Length	1 yd	= 0·9144 m		Length	1 ft	= 0·305 m
	1 m	= 1·0936 yd			1 m	= 3·281 ft
					1 in	= 25·4 mm
					1 mm	= 0·0394 in
				Area	1 yd²	= 0·836 m²
					1 m²	= 1·196 yd²
					1 ft²	= 0·093 m²
					1 m²	= 10·764 ft²
Force	1 lb f	= 4·448 N			1 in²	= 645·16 mm²
	1 N	= 0·225 lb f			1 mm²	= 0·00155 in²

Other, approximate, equivalents for dimensions referred to in this book

10 mm	= ⅜ in
100 mm	= 4 in
150 mm	= 6 in
600 mm	= 2 ft
1250 mm	= 4 ft
10 m	= 35 ft
15 m	= 50 ft

74

General index